DEFENDING OUR RAINFOREST

A GUIDE TO COMMUNITY BASED ECOTOURISM IN THE ECUADORIAN AMAZON

Rolf Wesche
Andy Drumm
with

Nicole Ayotte
Lindsay Collis
Sylvestre Fink
Isabelle Gariépy
Kimberley Horrocks
Carlos Landázuri
Nadine Nickner
Geneviève Renart
Sonia St-Michel
Octavio Yumbo
Rebecca Zalatan

Katherine Bemben
Marijo Cyr
Martin Gamache
Jonathan Godin
Cédric Jeanneret
Jo-Anne McArthur
Pablo Oleas
Hilary Stedwill
Danielle Trépanier
Sonia Wesche

Université d'Ottawa
University of Ottawa

Saving the Last Great Places

Embajada Británica
Quito

DEFENDING OUR RAINFOREST

A GUIDE TO COMMUNITY BASED ECOTOURISM IN THE ECUADORIAN AMAZON

Rolf Wesche
Andy Drumm

with

Nicole Ayotte
Lindsay Collis
Sylvestre Fink
Isabelle Gariépy
Kimberley Horrocks
Carlos Landázuri
Nadine Nickner
Geneviève Renart
Sonia St-Michel
Octavio Yumbo
Rebecca Zalatan

Katherine Bemben
Marijo Cyr
Martin Gamache
Jonathan Godin
Cédric Jeanneret
Jo-Anne McArthur
Pablo Oleas
Hilary Stedwill
Danielle Trépanier
Sonia Wesche

Embajada Británica
Quito

1999

DEFENDING OUR RAINFOREST
A Guide to Community Based Ecotourism in the Ecuadorian Amazon
Rolf Wesche and Andy Drumm

Copyright © 1999 by Acción Amazonía

1ra. Edición:
• Acción Amazonía
República E 7-320 y Diego de Almagro
Edificio Taurus Dpto. 1-A
Telf.: 225-907 / 234-994
Fax: 560-756
E-mail: accionamazonia@ecuadorexplorer.com
Quito-Ecuador

• Ediciones Abya-Yala
Av. 12 de octubre 14-30 y Wilson
Casilla 17-12-719
Telf.: 562-633 / 506-247
Fax: 506-255 / 506-267
E-mail: editorial@abya-yala.org
Quito-Ecuador
• University of Ottawa
• Embajada Británica Quito
• The Nature Conservancy

Autoedición:
Abya-Yala Editing
Quito-Ecuador

ISBN:
9978-04-560-0

Impresión:
Nina Comunicaciones
Quito-Ecuador

Impreso en Quito-Ecuador, 1999

TABLE OF CONTENTS

LIST OF MAPS

ACKNOWLEDGEMENTS

This book would not have seen the light of the jungle dawn if it had not been for the help of people and institutions too numerous to adequately acknowledge here.

We first and foremost are indebted to the 42 indigenous communities who received us with extraordinary hospitality, who taught us about their values and their way of life, and whom we shall not forget. Carlos Landazuri and Octavio Yumbo, Quichua of the Tena area were part of our team and became our friends. The indigenous organizations RICANCIE (Emilio Grefa, Tarquino Tapuy), ATACAPI Tours (José Gualinga, Martin Jovanov), OPIP (César Cerda), Unión Huacamayos (Benito Nantipa), SIONA-TOUR (Anibal Piaguaje, Miriam Ramirez) and ONHAE (Juan Huamoni, Nanto Huamoni), played a vital role in facilitating the team's access to their member communities. INEFAN (Arturo Ponce, Victor Hugo Vargas, Patricio Taco, Luis Borbor) facilitated access to protected areas.

The University of Ottawa (the Faculty of Arts, the Environmental Studies Program, the Student Federation of the Faculty of Arts, the Vice Rector of University Relations and Development) supported the field work of the research team and the preparation of the manuscript. The British Embassy in Quito, Abya Yala, The Ecotourism Society, PROBONA and The Nature Conservancy financed the publication of the English edition.

The opinions expressed in this book are the responsability of the authors. The support of the aforementioned organizations for this publication in no way implies responsability for its content.

Acción Amazonía provided office facilities, logistical support and communication with indigenous communities and organizations. The Gesellschaft für technische Zusammenarbeit (Hans Knoblauch of Proyecto Gran Sumaco) provided logistical and office support and financed the participation of Octavio Yumbo. The Universidad Andina Simon Bolívar in Quito (Raúl Mideros) provided computer facilities and working space at reduced rates. CANODROS provided a free visit to Kapawi Lodge. Pedro Katz and crew at Difoto in Quito worked exceptionally hard to meet our needs and deadlines. Bruce Robin of the University of Ottawa prepared the maps.

Other individuals who furthered the project in a variety of ways include Alejandro Argumendo (Cultural Survival Canada), Megan Epler Wood (TES), Daniel Kouperman (Kapawi-CANODROS), Kurt Kutay (Wildland Adventures), Sofia Darquea, Monica Paez (TROPIC Ecological Adventures), Pablo Oleas (Acción Amazonía), Richard Resl, Hans Christian Thiel (GTZ-Profors), and Mari Wesche.

Finally, a special thanks to the team of Environmental Studies and Geography students of the University of Ottawa who are listed as junior co-authors. Their dedication, creativity, enthusiasm and resilience made this project a particularly rewarding experience.

Rolf Wesche
Andy Drumm

PREFACE

For all that's been researched, written, spoken and broadcast about the Amazon rainforest these last ten years, one might be forgiven for thinking that it was all wrapped up, that with the word finally out about its enormous ecological value and cultural diversity, the world had finally come to its senses and had given it the protection it deserves and that the planet needs. Well, to our shame, the reality is quite different: the martyrdom of Chico Mendes and the demise of uncounted numbers of indigenous inhabitants, including entire cultures, have served as mere alarm calls ignored by a world that has difficulty waking up.

This vast forest where one hectare contains more tree species than the whole of North America, where a breathtaking knowledge of the medicinal and other utilitarian uses of plants is common to native peoples everywhere, where like humans, the jaguar, the scarlet macaw, the anaconda and freshwater dolphins represent the perfection of their evolutionary process, is being eroded, poisoned and consumed as we speak.

The pressures of population growth send landless farmers ever deeper into the forest, and the intolerable pressure of foreign debt payments forces desperate Latin American economies to sack their natural resources in a terrifyingly unsustainable fashion.

Those countries which have, in the face of these pressures, managed to truly protect any national parks or respect the integrity of any indigenous territories should be saluted for their foresight and for the enormous effort this requires. However, even the most cursory examination will reveal that even in these most ecologically and culturally valuable of areas, destructive and consumptive processes are at work.

In the Ecuadorian Amazon, it is undoubtedly the insatiable thirst for oil in the North and for export income in Ecuador which presents the greatest threat to environmental and cultural survival. But there is also an illicit timber industry and uncontrolled and poorly managed tourism to contend with.

Fortunately there are counter currents:

Recent years have seen the emergence of a stronger indigenous voice through the birth of a number of ethnicity-based and regional representative organizations. Simultaneously, the growth of environmental awareness has been shadowed by growing activism from urban-based non-governmental organizations (NGOs).

Conservationists and indigenous organizations, while sharing many common fundamental goals have, in the past, been largely unable to build alliances which last beyond single issue campaigns. The reasons for this have included a degree of mutual mistrust between conservationists, who are perceived to put plants and animals before human welfare, and indigenous people, who would appear to seek development without regard for the long term viability of our natural resources. Social, cultural and geographical distance as well as divisive strategies employed by those most threatened by the trend toward sustainable development has tended to contribute to the maintenance of a divide between these two sectors.

Acción Amazonía has been created in Ecuador by people with many years of experience in building solid bridges between environmentalists and indigenous communities and organizations. Indeed, our Foundation is a product of both sectors working in unison. We recognize that the natural areas of the Amazon cannot survive without the commitment of their indigenous inhabitants, just as the immensely rich diversity of Amazon culture cannot survive without pristine forests and rivers and abundant wildlife. However, in an era during which just two or three clans continue to roam the Ecuadorian rainforest without contact with the outside world and all remaining indigenous communities are to a greater or lesser degree irreversibly influenced by the expanding capitalist economy, it is untenable to demand their commitment to conservation while denying them access to the means of improving the quality of life at the community level.

Acción Amazonía supports practical projects which provide sustainable development alternatives for Ecuadorian Amazon communities while encouraging the rational use of resources at a time when outside pressures promote just the opposite.

Without the assurance of the continued existence of the rainforest habitat where the myths, legends and history of entire nations were born, not only will we lose the biological and genetic diversity of which it is made, but also the vast richness of knowledge, understanding and culture to which it has given life.

This guidebook is a contribution to our environmental and cultural goals of sustainable development. By facilitating a greater flow of interested Amazon visitors to those communities, and only those, who wish to receive them and who manage the operation, income is generated which allows the conservation of resources as well as encouraging respect for cultures which have been abused and denigrated for too long. What is more, the visitor will, through the unique experience of seeing the rainforest through the eyes of the people who live there, almost certainly gain insights which will make him or her a new ally in our common struggle to defend the Amazon.

Andy Drumm

FOREWORD

VISITING COMMUNITIES WITH RESPECT

Travelers take note! This guide to community based eco-tourism offers a unique introduction to important community projects that are eager to host you. If you travel with the right mind and in the right spirit, you can make an important contribution to conservation of the Amazon rainforest of Ecuador.

But be aware! You must follow the instructions in this book for responsible traveling carefully. As this perceptive guide notes, the level of exposure to Western culture and tourists varies greatly in these communities. Check your Nikes, Walkman and other brand name conveniences in Quito. Travel simply. Try to expand your worldview. Concentrate on learning from your hosts. Save your globe-trotting travel tales for friends and family. This may be your only chance to be in this unique place, with this one community. BE with them.

As the new millenium dawns, an extraordinary window of opportunity exists in Ecuador. Every year more travelers visit the rainforest, and for the first time ecotourism is being recognized as a valid tool for economic development of Ecuador's Amazon region (the Oriente). The Ecotourism Society defines ecotourism as, "responsible travel to natural areas that conserves the environment and sustains the wellbeing of local people." Ecotourism can be offered by multi-million dollar companies or by local communities, as long as proper criteria are applied. In the Oriente, an extraordinary number of community based ecotourism projects have flowered. This type of locally based tourism brings income directly to local families, subsidizing a sustainable way of life that has existed in the region for thousands of years. While it can never be the sole source of family income in the region, community based ecotourism can help validate continuing conservation of millions of hectares of rainforest in indigenous territories and conservation areas. It is a crucial tool to help rule out the usual progression of economic development that places severe environmental stress on protected zones, such as logging, oil exploitation and market-oriented agriculture.

For the traveler it can be confusing to select an ecotourism experience – so many are being sold from the most posh to the most basic. Community based ecotourism projects are often difficult to find, and until now, the information about them was unreliable. The significance of supporting community based tourism projects can easily be lost on the average traveler, yet such travel decisions do have an important social and economic impact. Communities living in rainforest ecosystems are entering the market economy for a reason. They need funds to buy goods and services. Even in the remotest part of the Amazon, children are going to school and their parents need to buy school supplies. Health care is no longer handled entirely locally, and emergency care and transport to modern hospitals is now considered to be a necessity.

I once traveled with a Siecoya *shaman* on an airplane to Quito. I sat with him in the airport in Lago Agrio, with children crowding all around us, as he pulled on a huge set of sneakers over his normally bare, toughened feet. Having stayed in his home, I knew how antagonistic he was towards the commercial oil economy which has invaded the Cuyabeno region. I heard him speak seriously of relocating his family away from all

Westernized influences. His family was largely self-sufficient, living with little impact, utilizing the rich game and fisheries of the region. He was a specialist in medicinal plants, and a well-known healer. Yet, he did not see the contradiction of flying to Quito when he needed to get specialized medical care. Most families in the Oriente need less than $500 per year to support their needs. With the basic necessities of modern life met, they opt to live largely as their parents and grandparents have done, in harmony with the environment. This is the story of life in the Ecuadorian Amazon today.

It is a rich place, known not only as one of the most biodiverse regions of the planet, but also as remarkably culturally preserved. The indigenous people have a long history of fighting for territorial rights, and winning. This is not common in most parts of Latin America, or the world for that matter. As this book explains, more than one third of the Oriente is now recognized as indigenous territory, and the indigenous federations have declared that they are the rightful guardians of the entire Ecuadorian Amazon.

There are millions of hectares of unbroken rainforest in the Oriente and small populations of people who need only the smallest subsidy to live healthy, sustainable lives. Small-scale businesses, that are community owned, and community operated make perfect sense here. Thirty-eight community based ecotourism projects are reviewed in this book; each managed with a mind to primarily benefit local residents. These projects represent an extraordinary diversity of community based ecotourism opportunities that is presently unrivaled in any other region of the world. For the first time, this well-designed book offers the latest compiled information on community based ecotourism in

Ecuador – an extraordinary service to the traveler and an important contribution to conservation of the region.

Unfortunately, most of these projects are very little known. It has been a struggle for many of the communities listed here to compete. Their knowledge of marketing is understandably limited. While most do not need a tremendous flow of tourists, they need a small but regular clientele to depend on. In fact, most communities should not be seeking more than a limited number of visitors in order to maintain cultural integrity. But expectations are important, and ecotourism projects, even at a very small scale, can be viewed as pivotal to the future of local families. Disappointment at the lack of sustained market success is particularly damaging to community morale. If local leaders believe ecotourism does not deliver adequate benefits they turn elsewhere, and the alternatives are often not ideal.

On my visit to the Siecoya on the Aguarico, I saw dozens of Siecoya workers being ferried in spanking, clean orange overalls and white hard hats downriver to a new oil camp. Efforts to launch an ecotourism project in the community had not reaped significant profits, and community members had been easily lured by the Oil Company to work on crews testing for oil. If oil was found, an extension of the pipeline would be built with roads directly into the center of Siecoya territory – a prospect that would clearly change the lives of this small forest tribe forever.

Change comes, and global economic development and the creation of a global culture may be inevitable. But in the face of these nearly unstoppable trends, areas like the Ecuadorian Oriente are becoming increasingly precious. They need to be protected not only for their rainforests. They need to be protected because human understanding of how to live sustainably still resides in these living cultures. Visiting community based ecotourism projects provides the traveler with a window to vanishing wisdom. This is why we must go to these communities with the utmost respect. It may be a key to our survival.

Megan Epler Wood
President of The Ecotourism Society

For more information on responsible travel contact The Ecotourism Society, P.O. Box 755, N. Bennington, VT 05257, USA. Tel: 802-447-2121. Fax: 802-447-3770. E-mail: eco-mail@ecotourism.org. Internet: www.ecotourism.org.

I
INTRODUCTION

Ecuador's Amazon region (Maps 1, 2) -the **Oriente**- has attracted nature tourists since the late 1960s. In the 1990s tourist numbers have begun to approach those of the Galápagos Islands, Ecuador's premier ecotourism destination. Most of this clientele is serviced by some 30 jungle lodges and over 70 independent guides. The former are best described in <u>The New Key Guide to Ecuador and the Galápagos</u> (Pearson and Middleton 1997), the latter in <u>The Lonely Planet Travel Survival Kit: Ecuador and the Galápagos Islands</u> (Rachowiecki 1997), the <u>Let's Go: Ecuador and the Galápagos Islands</u> guidebook (Veltri 1998) and the <u>South American Handbook</u> (Box 1997).

While many of the lodges and an increasing number of the guides observe adequate environmental standards, their treatment of the local indigenous peoples is often questionable. The following practices apply in many, though by no means all cases: Indigenous labor is employed in low paid, unqualified jobs. Training opportunities are limited. Indigenous settlements are visited intrusively and without adequate compensation. Tourist visits and resulting income are unpredictable. Handicrafts are undervalued.

Largely as a result of these shortcomings of conventional naturetourism, a new type of ecotourism arose in the Oriente during the 1990s: indigenous **community based ecotourism (CBE)**. CBE encompasses enterprises which are located in indigenous territories and which are owned and/or operated by indigenous people. These may include indigenous organizations, communities, individuals, or families, as well as joint ventures with non-indigenous partners. CBE projects show the Amazon from an indigenous perspective and support indigenous environmental conservation and cultural survival through indigenous control and the retention of tourism income in the communities.

So far CBE has been completely neglected in the tourism literature on Ecuador. In 1995, one of the main authors of this book and a group of Geography students of the University of Ottawa published a first inventory of CBE enterprises as part of a comprehensive guidebook of Napo province, the most important ecotourism region of the Oriente (The Ecotourist's Guide to the Ecuadorian Amazon: Napo Province, Wesche et al. 1995). Since then CBE enterprises have mushroomed and spread over three of the five Oriente provinces. In fact, the Oriente is now the leading CBE region of its size in the tropics.

This guidebook describes the CBE phenomenon in the context of Ecuador's Amazon frontier development and provides a complete inventory of CBE enterprises. It is the first comprehensive inventory of CBE in a major region of the developing countries.

The guidebook seeks to educate the responsible traveler rather than embellishing the truth in order to lure innocent readers to a mythical destination. Thus no story of "noble savages" living in unbroken blissful harmony with their environment is found in these pages. For such images the reader is referred to coffee table books and the advertising of ecotourism operators with dubious ethics. With few exceptions, the indigenous peoples of the Oriente have long been subjected to Western influences. In fact, they have adopted CBE in reaction and adaptation to these outside influences. Where indigenous peoples have not yet been impacted and have not chosen tourism as a development option, the responsible traveler is advised to leave them alone.

This guidebook presents the unembellished reality of wrenching changes, and of indigenous peoples groping for sustainable development in their threatened habitat within the constraints and possibilities imposed by the modern world. It relies on the discriminating and sympathetic reading of the responsible traveler, who is not only concerned with the environment but also with the social implications of travel. Tourism can be a constructive, mutually beneficial exchange between the traveler and the host community; or it can be an exploitative relationship which degrades the host community and is of questionable value to the tourist. IF YOUR OBJECTIVE IS TO SQUEEZE THE CHEAPEST TRAVEL ARRANGEMENT OUT OF THE LOCALS, PLEASE DO NOT READ FURTHER - OR RATHER DO READ FURTHER AND REFLECT.

The book is based on field work by the main authors and 18 advanced undergraduate students of Environmental Studies and Geography at the University of Ottawa, Canada. Rolf Wesche first visited the Oriente as a backpacker in 1964 and returned for extended periods of research and field study courses on six other occasions. Andy Drumm has been intimately involved in ecotourism and indigenous development in the Oriente from his base in Quito since 1990. The students have contributed their fresh perspective, enthusiasm for appropriate development and extraordinary wilderness skills after undergoing a year of preparation. All localities mentioned were surveyed in May and June, 1998.

The book is divided into three main parts. The first (chapters II-III) briefly introduces those indigenous language groups *(nacionalidades)* which currently practice CBE, as well as the natural environment and territorial division of their home – the Oriente.

The second part (chapters IV-VI) situates CBE in the context of Ecuador's Amazon frontier occupation and identifies its role within a new indigenous development strategy. It furthermore characterizes CBE and provides guidance for the responsible traveler.

The third part (chapters VII-X) provides a complete inventory of CBE projects organized by subregion. Within each subregion CBE projects are presented in order of increasing difficulty of access (implying increasing distance, cost, logistical difficulty and time required) from the principal urban center.

Key features of the individual CBE projects are presented in table form (Appendix 1) and CBE locations are identified in foldout maps 3-5 (Appendix 2). The final part of the book also contains tips for travelers to the Oriente, a glossary of acronyms and uncommon terms, an annotated bibliography with indications where relevant literature can be obtained, and the main authors' addresses.

II
THE INDIGENOUS NATIONALITIES
OF THE ORIENTE

The protagonists of this book, the indigenous peoples *(pueblos indígenas)* of the Ecuadorian Amazon, started the community based ecotourism (CBE) movement in Ecuador. They think of themselves as nationalities *(nacionalidades)* on the basis of language affiliation. Nationalities include the lowland Quichua Shuar, Achuar, Huaorani, Cofan, Siona, Siecoya and Záparo (Map 1). Collectively, they identify themselves as *"indígenas"* of the Ecuadorian Amazon and distinguish themselves from the far more numerous *indígenas* of the Ecuadorian Highlands *(Sierra)*. They are organized at the community and nationality level, and are members of the umbrella organization CONFENIAE (Confederation of Indigenous Nationalities of the Ecuadorian Amazon). CONFENIAE, in turn, is part of CONAIE (Confederation of Indigenous Nationalities of Ecuador) and COICA (Coordinating Body of Indigenous Peoples of the Amazon Basin) which covers seven Amazonian countries.

At the national scale and the scale of the entire Amazon Basin, the *indígenas* of the Oriente have played a leadership role in the indigenous movement which is out of proportion with their numbers. This increases the importance of the CBE experience in the Ecuadorian Amazon as a model for other regions. Since indigenous leaders from the Oriente are prominent in COICA, they have started to diffuse ideas to incipient CBE projects in other Amazonian countries. Contacts have also been established with Central America.

The Oriente is as distinct from the rest of the country as are its indigenous inhabitants. It is composed of Ecuador's five east-

Map 1. Indigenous Territories in the Oriente

Map 2. Principal Nature Reserves in the Oriente

Line of Rio de Janeiro Protocol of 1942

LEGEND

1. Cayambe-Coca Ecological Reserve
2. Cuyabeno Wildlife Reserve
3. Antisana Ecological Reserve
4. Sumaco-Galeras National Park
5. Limoncocha Biological Reserve
6. Yasuní National Park
7. Llanganates National Park
8. Sangay National Park
9. Podocarpus National Park

ernmost provinces: Sucumbíos, Napo, Pastaza, Morona-Santiago and Zamora-Chinchipe. (As this book goes to press, a new province "Orellana" with its capital Coca, has been created from the eastern part of Napo province). These are separated from the Highlands and the Coast by the daunting eastern range of the Andes, which is only traversed by five dirt roads.

Since it is the resource frontier region of the country, the Oriente has witnessed dramatic changes over the last three decades. These include road construction, oil exploitation, agricultural settlement, lumber extraction and non-indigenous controlled tourism. The impact on the indígenas has been substantial. All indigenous nationalities of the Oriente thus are societies in transition, from traditional isolation to partial integration into the country's frontier society.

These groups, throughout history, have been mobile within the rainforest. With continuing pressures on their land and the slow process of recognition of indigenous territories, groups continue to shift in space; thus a clear historical association between a group and a territory is difficult to establish. The larger ethnic groups, i.e. the Quichua and the Shuar, serve as models for indigenous organization and political representation. For the smaller groups (e.g. Cofan, Záparo) proper organization and representation as an entity is somewhat more difficult, but nonetheless crucial to find beneficial solutions as they integrate themselves into the frontier society.

The purpose of this chapter is to briefly introduce those indigenous nationalities which are involved in CBE. This excludes from consideration the Shuar (Map 1) and consequently also the southern provinces of Morona-Santiago and Zamora-Chinchipe where CBE has not yet made an appearance.

QUICHUA

The Quichua *(Runa)* of the Oriente are related to the Quichua of the Andean Highlands, who began to adopt the Quichua language during the Inca Empire. Anthropologists believe that the Quichua language and associated cultural traits were introduced to the rainforest tribes from the Andes during the colonial period. The Quichua are now the most numerous of the Oriente's indigenous nationalities and it is possible to distinguish between two distinct groups: the Canelos and the Quijos. It is believed that the Canelos Quichua are the result of a fusion with the Achuar and the Záparo in the area of Pastaza province. The Quijos Quichua occupy the basins of the Napo, Aguarico, San Miguel and Putumayo Rivers *(Ríos)*. The two groups tend to mix in the northwestern part of Pastaza province. The culture as well as the language of the Quichua has absorbed various cultures of the region like the Yumbos or the Záparo. Acculturation continues as is illustrated by the fact that all language groups use Quichua words such as *shigra, chicha* and *cushma,* though their language contains appropriate terms. In spite of their diverse origins, the Quichua of the Oriente form a nationality comprised of approximately 90 000 members who share a common culture.

Traditionally, the Quichua were organized in *"muntuns";* residential groups varying in size which were centered around a headman or *shaman.* With the death of the group headmen, some families dissolved and some regrouped, making it difficult for outsiders to identify their precise relationships. At present, traditional organizations have been transformed into more formal ones. These groups have enabled the indigenous people to reach common objectives such as the defense of their territory and interests.

In the past, the territory of the Quijos Quichua has been limited by colonization, agro-industry, the petroleum industry and national parks and reserves. These different influences have pushed them towards the east, deeper into the rainforest onto lands of other indigenous groups. The Canelos Quichua, by contrast, have managed to hang on to most of their territory in a single block (Maps 1, 5).

The Quichua are perhaps best distinguished by their renowned ceramics, which are beautifully adorned with colored decorations and traditional symbols. They are used to serve *chicha,* a common drink made with fermented *yuca* (or other starchy food crops). Pottery work is generally done by the ones who hold the best knowledge of the symbolism of the universe, most often the wives or sisters of *shamans,* who are thought to be able to best capture this sacred imagery through their art. Contemporary designs are also incorporated into the ceramics due to the increasing influence of outside cultures.

Modern trends are also apparent in the dress of the Quichua of the Oriente, although cultural manifestations such as language, cuisine and traditional celebrations have remained mostly intact. The effect of their forced integration into modern society has, to an extent, promoted their organization at different levels, especially in the ecotourism industry. In fact, 72 percent of the CBE projects in the Oriente are in Quichua areas. The ability of the Quichua to maintain their customs, traditional medicinal practices and widespread use of their language, despite outside influences, has provided members with a solid and dynamic cultural identity. They have created several organizations to represent their interests: FCUNAE in the lower Napo, FOIN in the upper Napo and OPIP in Pastaza.

SIONA AND SIECOYA

The Siona and Siecoya (often spelled Secoya) speak close-ly related dialects. Belonging to the western Tucanoan language group, they are frequently referred to as "Siona-Siecoya". The cultural patterns of these two ethnic groups are similar and inter-marriage is common. In Ecuador, the Siona population consists of 200 inhabitants, while the Siecoya are comprised of 300 people. Together, they hold three parcels of land along the Ríos Aguarico and Cuyabeno of Sucumbíos province and some groups related to them occupy neighboring areas of Colombia and Peru. In fact, many Ecuadorian Siecoya consider the Río Lagartococha area which straddles the Peruvian boundary as their ancestral home-land, and are pursuing a land claim in that area. Similarly, the Colombian Siona are finding refuge from the violence in their homeland by joining their relatives in the Cuyabeno Wildlife Reserve of Ecuador. The early Franciscans and Jesuits called them *"Encabellados"* because of their long hair. In the nineteenth cen-tury, travelers called them *"Piojé"* (meaning "there is none"), since this was the indigenous people's response to requests for food. Today, they are no longer referred to in these terms.

The Siona and Siecoya communities have traditionally set-tled in scattered groups along small streams such as the Ríos Cuyabeno, Eno and Shushufundi (tributaries of the Río Aguarico southeast of Lago Agrio). Families commonly resided in large, oval-shaped communal houses with dirt floors. While the head-men and *shamans* looked after the wellbeing of the group, other community members *(socios)* formed the basic unit of production and consumption. Land clearing and gardening was done jointly among the men.

The fruits of the harvest were prepared in a communal area and shared equally among community members. The Siona and Siecoya often made use of the *achiote* plant (whose small red seeds contain a scarlet-red dye) for face painting, rituals and special occasions. The pigment was traditionally used in puberty rituals, war ceremonies, weddings, and to paint the faces of the dead before burial.

In their vision of the universe, the Siona and Siecoya distinguish three separate spheres of existence: Matemo, the sky; Yeja, "the land where we live"; and Gimocopain, "the world under our feet". According to Siona and Siecoya legends, their people are descendants of the inhabitants of Gimocopain, from whom they supposedly inherited the appearance of monkeys.

Acculturation has been significant, and is especially noticeable in terms of building material, house type, religious values and, to a lesser degree in settlement patterns, kinship and subsistence economy. For example, recent generations favor smaller elevated houses and live more individual lifestyles than their forebears. Their territory is now shared with settlers, African oil palm plantations and oil companies. Not many *shamans* remain.

The Siona communities seem to be the more organized of these two ethnic groups and they are putting these skills into practice through their involvement in CBE. They have initiated a central organization, SIONATOUR, to facilitate coordination among the three Siona communities that offer ecotourism. OISE (Siecoya) and ONISE (Siona) are their representative organizations.

COFAN

The Cofan people formerly inhabited an extensive territory in the Aguarico watershed from the foothills of the Andes to the confluence of the Ríos Aguarico and Zábalo. They have been more strongly impacted by the oil industry and settlers than any other group.

Their traditional subsistence economy was based on hunting, fishing, gathering and the growing of *plátanos* and *yuca*. The traditional organization was characterized by family groups, the central figure being the *shaman* who was in charge of the well-being of the group. The key to inner knowledge, according to the Cofan, (like many other groups of the Amazon), was by consumption of *yagé*. This hallucinogenic plant induces magical visions filled with meaningful symbols. Preparation for the ceremony takes almost one full day. The ritual begins at 6 pm, when the jungle is full of the chirping of crickets and the eerie evening lighting gives a mystical ambiance.

The traditional clothing and body ornaments of the Cofan are both distinctive and elaborate. Men's attire consists of open tunics and a colorful feathered crown for special occasions. Women typically dress in a blouse and skirt (introduced by the missionaries), with necklaces and wristbands made of jungle beads, animal teeth and toucan beaks. Even today, some of the older women and men don pierced ears and nose with ornaments of feathers and flowers.

In 1602, the Jesuit mission established the first Cotan village by the name of "San Pedro de los Cofanes" along the Río Aguarico, upriver from the community of Sinangüe (Map 3). The site of San Pedro is now a colonist *(colono)* village named Puerto

Libre, traversed by a new highway which is being built by a
Brazilian multinational company. This example sadly reflects the
unfolding fate of the Cofan.

The 500 remaining Ecuadorian Cofan are now dispersed in
five communities: Doveno, Dureno and Zábalo along the Río
Aguarico; Sinangüe and Chandia Na'en (or Bermejo) in the
Andean foothills. OINCE, the Cofan organization, is weakened by
the lack of good communication between the five communities.
Three of these settlements presently grow cash crops such as rice,
coffee and maize for sale in nearby colonist towns, and produce
typical handicrafts (artesanía) such as hammocks and handbags
(shigras). Another 200 Cofan live in Colombia along the Ríos San
Miguel and Guamuez.

Three of the communities mentioned above offer ecotourism to varying degrees. Zábalo and Dureno have had a long
history of tourism, and the former can serve as a model of successful CBE. Sinangüe has shown some potential for ecotourism
and interest in adopting such an enterprise. Chandia Na'en has
great potential for trekking through spectacular terrain.

HUAORANI

Although they are often referred to as "Auca" (Quichua for "savages"), in their language, the word Huaorani actually means "people". They historically considered themselves as "people" and designated everyone else as *"cowode"*, meaning non-human. Their language is unrelated to that of any other indigenous group of the Oriente and their ethnic origins remain to be clarified. Still today, the Huaorani are reasonably mobile and occupy a large territory located mostly in interfluvial zones between the Río Napo to the north and the Río Curaray to the south. The first Huaorani protectorate was created in 1983 and the much larger Huaorani Ethnic Reserve was established in 1990. These have somewhat restricted Huaorani mobility. Among the indigenous nationalities the Huaorani have, nevertheless, the least densely populated territory and are presently numbered at 1 500 to 2 000 persons who inhabit 24 communities. Three of these are outside the Huaorani Reserve within Yasuní National Park.

The Huaorani identify themselves as the fiercest and most indestructible group in the Amazon, as long as there is abundance in the forest. The Huaorani are known to be skilled hunters and retain their reputation as warriors. Like many Amazon nationalities they consider all human deaths as having been caused by other humans and requiring revenge. This contributed to almost permanent conflicts between clans in the past. Their reputation for fierceness has served the Huaorani well in protecting their extensive homeland.

The Huaorani hold a great appreciation for hunting: in their vision of the universe they perceive paradise as being a never-ending hunting land. They also depend on a system of "*chacras*" (small-scale clearings used for subsistence agriculture) as a source of food. Their strongest value is that of family solidarity and sharing among the people. In the past, men could marry up to five women, but due to the influence of missionaries, the newer generation tends to marry only once. A traditional household consists of about 12 members. The open fire in the dwelling is a very important symbol of the Huaorani lifestyle. It not only provides a constant source of heat and light, but also serves for cooking and for warding off insects. The informal education system of the Huaorani is primarily through example, with the elders passing on their skills and wisdom to the younger generation. Some of the elders still wear the typical "*Komi*" (traditional hip cord). Large ear piercings and long hair complete the traditional Huaorani attire.

Oil exploration and exploitation in and near Huaorani territory has resulted in significant erosion of their way of life. Some communities have moved deeper into the forest to avoid all contact with the outside world while others have adopted activities such as ecotourism to maintain control over their land. Consequently, many Huaorani have gradually organized themselves into effective political groups. However, their attitude has always been that they were never defeated or conquered and will remain independent. Three Huaorani groups have so far escaped contact with Western civilization: the Tagaeri, the Taromenane and the Oñamenane. ONHAE is the youngest of the Oriente's representative organizations.

ACHUAR

The Achuar are part of the Jívaro linguistic family as are the Shuar (the second most populous indigenous group of the Oriente) and the Shiwiar. They now occupy a large area of Ecuador and Peru along the Río Pastaza, with 5 000 Achuar on the Ecuadorian side (Maps 1, 5). Achuar and Shuar have been involved in historical internal wars that ended with the intrusion of outsiders, such as missionaries and colonists. Until the late 1960s, the Achuar had not been exposed to the Western world because of the difficult access and the group's reputation as warriors. Facial war paint is one of the most impressive features of the Achuar culture. These designs serve various purposes such as hiding the fear of the warriors, making them appear more aggressive, and protecting them during battle. In the late 1960s, missionaries established their first contact with the Achuar people. Since then, various aspects of this indigenous group's culture have been modified under their influence.

Myths and beliefs have been extremely important for the Achuar people in keeping their traditions alive. This is especially important nowadays, with the growing pressures and impact of Western society. The Achuar believe that their contacts with multiple spirits have given them the guidelines for a harmonious relationship with the rainforest and its creatures. They communicate with the spirits of the jungle through sacred songs, dreams and with hallucinogenic plants like many other indigenous groups. Some of their beliefs were considered diabolic by missionaries in the past, and have been largely suppressed as a result.

The traditional settlement pattern of the Achuar is in a dispersed fashion throughout the forest, with extended families generally living together under one roof. Men are allowed to have several wives and the size of the household depends largely on the number of wives. The living quarters are divided according to sex into two separate designated areas, a practice which is still observed today. The male section *("tankamash")* is generally off limits to women unless they are serving *chicha* or food to guests. The *"ekent"* is primarily the women's reserved space where only the master of the household is allowed to enter.

Hunting, fishing, horticulture and gathering form the basis of the traditional economy of the Achuar. Today, they also practice small-scale market-oriented agricultural activities. Nowadays, with the construction of airstrips, some families have organized themselves around the runways. Among other changes, ecotourism has flourished. For example, six Achuar communities have become involved in a successful joint venture called Kapawi Lodge. FINAE (Federation of Ecuadorian Achuar Nationalities), the well-organized Achuar association, contemplates further development of ecotourism in the future.

ZÁPARO

Much of the existing anthropological literature does not distinguish the Záparo among the indigenous groups of the Ecuadorian Amazon, since they and their culture have been largely absorbed by the Canelos Quichua. The remainder live in Pastaza province, along the Río Conambo in the remote communities of Llanchamacocha and Jandiayacu (Map 5). These communities are presently a part of the ATACAPI Tours program developed by OPIP (Organization of Indigenous Peoples of Pastaza). Today, only 24 people know the original Záparo dialect. According to registries of CONAIE, the total Záparo population is estimated at 40. The Záparo people were strong in war, but disappeared due to internal conflicts caused by witchcraft and sickness introduced by missionaries, settlers and rubber tappers.

Both settlements are located a week's walk from the nearest main road and thus access is mainly by plane (via two airstrips). The communities are still traditionally organized with dispersed houses, and are a one-day trip by dugout paddle canoe from one another. The domiciles are surrounded by crops such as bananas, *plátanos* and *yuca*. A subsistence mentality persists although occasional flights in and out of the communities allow for some exchange.

While traditional war weapons such as the lance and shield have disappeared, the Záparo culture remains rich in handicrafts and art with ceramics, basket-making, music and symbolic drawings.

Recently, the larger community of Llanchamacocha completed the construction of a new school. The airstrip has also been extended, in order to facilitate transportation to and from the area. The remaining Záparo are now increasingly conscious of their absorption by the Quichua, and are forming their own association. They see ecotourism as a unique opportunity to revive Záparo traditions.

Petroglyph
(K. Bemben)

III
THE GEOGRAPHICAL CONTEXT

The Oriente makes up almost half of Ecuador. From north to south, it is divided into the provinces of Sucumbíos, Napo, Pastaza, Morona-Santiago and Zamora-Chinchipe. The two southernmost provinces are disregarded in this book, since they do not yet contain CBE enterprises. Each of the three northern provinces, which constitute the study area, stretches some 250 to 300 kilometers (km) from the crest of the eastern range of the Andes to the contested lowland jungle boundary with Peru (Map 2).

The region has a sparse network of dirt roads which are muddy when wet and dusty when dry. Only a few kilometers of road near the main towns are paved. Nevertheless, the roads are reasonably predictable except when the occasional landslide occurs. All main towns are connected by bus systems, with buses running several times daily.

In the west, one road axis follows the foot of the Andes (Map 2). It is connected to the highland cities of Quito and Ambato (via Baños) by two spectacular access roads across the eastern range of the Andes. The main tourist gateway centres of Tena, Puerto Misahuallí (on a side road east of Tena), and Puyo are located in the Andean foothills along this western axis. In Sucumbíos and Napo, a simple road network extends from the western axis into the lowlands. The oil towns and tourist gateways of Lago Agrio and Coca are located at strategic junctions of this network.

Beyond the limited areas which are directly accessible by road, the main form of transportation is large outboard powered dugout canoes or chartered aircraft. In Sucumbíos and Napo provinces where roadheads reach the predictably navigable Ríos Aguarico and Napo and their tributaries, canoe transport predominates. In Pastaza, by contrast, single engine aircraft chartered in Shell (near Puyo) are the prevailing means of access to outlying locations.

Petroglyph
(K. Bemben)

PHYSICAL ENVIRONMENT

Since the Oriente ranges from the Andes to the Amazon lowlands, this region contains a striking variety of environments. Its western limits are in cold, wind-swept *páramos* (high-altitude grasslands between 3 400 and 4 500 meters (m) elevation). The *páramos*, in turn, are studded by six spectacular ice-capped volcanoes which rise above 5 000 m. From the *páramos* the rugged, dissected eastern slopes of the Andes descend rapidly through the cloud forest (2 500 to 3 400 m elevation). Here, dripping tree crowns laden with mosses, lichens and epiphytes loom among swirling mist and clouds. The lower slopes (600 to 2 500 m elevation) are covered by lower montane forests in which tree ferns are prominent. This is an area of deeply-incised valleys, clear rushing streams and an abundance of waterfalls.

Some 30 km east of the Andes, a parallel lower mountain range, completely shrouded in cloud forests and lower montane forests, extends through Sucumbíos and Napo. It is dominated by the Reventador (3 562 m), Pan de Azúcar (3 482 m), and Sumaco (3 900 m) volcanoes whose peaks rise into the *páramo,* and the Cordillera Galeras (1 589 m). The whole area between 600 and 3 400 m in elevation (which includes the eastern slope of the Andes, the parallel range and the piedmont) is referred to as the "high jungle" *(selva alta).*

Beyond the piedmont and parallel range extends the humid tropical lowland forest *(selva baja),* which covers more than half of the Oriente. Here the land gradually drops from 600 to 200 m elevation. In spite of low elevation, most of the land - particularly in the west - has a rolling or dissected topography, with only limited areas being permanently swampy or subject to inundation. Trees are taller than in the *selva alta* and occasional giants, notably *ceibos,* emerge above the canopy. Undergrowth is more limited than in the *selva alta.* This makes it easier to walk beyond cut trails and observe under the canopy.

Once they have traversed the Andean piedmont and parallel range, the rivers widen, leaving behind their last gravel deposits and rapids while still within view of the mountains. They become navigable by motorized canoe and start to lazily wind their way toward the Peruvian boundary and the Atlantic Ocean 4 000 km beyond. Along their lower courses, some of these rivers are linked to picturesque lagoons *(lagunas).* These generally have particularly abundant wildlife and serve as major tourist attractions.

For most of the Oriente, the drier season *(verano)* extends from late August to January, December and January generally being the driest months of the year. The rainy season *(invierno)* usually peaks in June and July; however, weather patterns have been irregular in recent years, probably in part as the result of the deforestation which follows in the wake of the oil industry.

Throughout the rainy season, periods of rainfall are interspersed with sunny periods. Despite the downpours, the rainy period is attractive to tourists since the weather is cooler, canoe travel is facilitated by higher water levels in lesser rivers and lagoons, and bothersome sandflies are less prominent than in the drier season. Generally cloudy weather and extended periods of moderate rainfall characterise the *selva alta.* The *selva baja,* by contrast, typically has shorter, heavier downpours interspersed with sunny skies. Throughout the Oriente the visitor will be faced with spectacular, ever-changing displays of cloud formations.

THE DIVISION OF SPACE: SETTLERS, INDIGENOUS PEOPLES, AND NATURE RESERVES

Until the 1960s, the Oriente was the largely unchallenged domain of the lowland indigenous nations. The lowland Quichua predominate in the three northernmost provinces which form the subject of this book, while the Shuar predominate in Morona-Santiago and Zamora-Chinchipe. The bulk of the Quichua population is concentrated in the western half of the Oriente, but scattered settlements have been established all the way to the Peruvian boundary. The less numerous Achuar, Huaorani, Cofan, Siona and Siecoya, as well as the remnants of Záparo and Shiwiar occupy more remote locations farther to the east.

In the early 1960s, the area had very low population densities and with few exceptions, was covered by primary forest. The indigenous territories were neither clearly delimited nor officially recognized. In fact, the government considered most of the area as unused public domain.

This situation changed rapidly after 1967 due to oil discoveries and expanded road construction, which particularly affected Sucumbíos and Napo provinces. Along the new roads, settlers from the Andes and the Coast established family farms with government encouragement. The settler encroachment, in turn, forced some indigenous populations to move to remoter areas in search of living space. This process was further encouraged by the high natural growth rates of the Quichua and Shuar.

Initially, the government failed to delimit and protect indigenous territories and sensitive environments against settler encroachment. Its record improved substantially in the last two decades, largely due to pressure from indigenous organizations, environmental NGOs (non-governmental organizations), foreign aid institutions and the burgeoning ecotourism industry. Presently only very limited areas are slated for the further expansion of settlement, and the government, with assistance from the *indígenas* and NGOs, is increasingly effective in preventing settlers from squatting in areas designated for other purposes. As a result, the Oriente has now reached a reasonably stable three-fold division of space between settlers, indigenous people and nature reserves (Maps 1, 2).

Settler Areas: Settlers tend to dominate in urban centres and along major roads. They generally control the service facilities, the most accessible lands and the best soils for agriculture. Thus, the ecotourist normally first comes into contact with them when arriving in the tourism staging centres or when traveling along the road system.

Settler-dominated areas have relatively high population densities, with a typical lot size of 50 hectares. The main exception is a group of three large oil palm plantations in the vicinity of Shushufindi and Coca. Only small patches of primary forest with relatively few mammals remain in these regions. Consequently, they play only a limited role as ecotourism destinations. Despite this fact, the landscape in these areas is often a visually appealing mix of pastures, fields, trees and forest patches, in which a variety of bird life can be observed.

Indigenous Territories: Mostly since 1992, extensive areas have been legalized or at least formally recognized as indigenous territories. In these areas the ownership is normally communal. Member families are attributed lots for their use, typically along a river, where they practice small scale agriculture, mainly for purposes of family subsistence. The remaining community lands are typically set aside as a reserve for future settlement, hunting, gathering and - increasingly - ecotourism.

Though they have shrunk from their former extent, and in spite of recent population growth, the indigenous territories have generally low population densities and their forest cover remains largely intact. Thus indigenous territories are frequently attractive ecotourism destinations.

Nature Reserves: Nature reserves (also referred to as "protected areas") occupy most of the remainder of the Oriente and represent the region's high profile ecotourism attractions - though only a minority of tourists set foot in them because of their remoteness or their difficult terrain. The most important reserves, which are designated for a high level of protection because of their biodiversity, appear in Map 2. They can be divided into two types.

The western set covers the crest and slopes of the Andes as well as the outlying parallel range of Sucumbíos and Napo. These reserves include Cayambe-Coca, Antisana, Sumaco-Galeras, and Llanganates. Only sturdy trekkers will penetrate their challenging terrain. The eastern nature reserves - Cuyabeno, Limoncocha and Yasuní, by contrast, are lowland areas laced with slow flowing rivers, lagoon complexes and swamps. Access to these reserves is mainly by outboard powered canoe. In addition to these high profile regions, other areas have been set aside as protection forests as well.

The indigenous peoples are well positioned to play a role in the ecotourism development and management of these nature reserves since in many cases their territories abut against them, forming a buffer against settler encroachment. The relatively recent designation of protected areas means that they are largely superimposed on indigenous territories.

INEFAN (The Ecuadorian Institute of Forestry, Natural Areas and Wildlife) is the government authority charged with the conservation of the nature reserves, the monitoring of tourist use and the collection of entrance fees. The money earned from these fees is essential for the conservation of these largely underfunded areas. Staff shortages and inadequate funding of INEFAN have encouraged indigenous organizations to seek an increased role in the protection of such areas.

IV
FROM DEPENDENCY TOWARD SELF RELIANCE: THE HISTORICAL CONTEXT AND ORIGINS OF COMMUNITY BASED ECOTOURISM

Community based ecotourism is part of a recent movement by the indigenous nations of the Oriente toward more self reliant development. Similar movements currently exist in many developing regions of the world. This movement is a reaction against increasingly disruptive outside influences as well as an attempt to capitalize on new opportunities. A brief review of the historical and contemporary context is given here to facilitate the appreciation of this movement toward self reliance, and the role of CBE within it.

DEPENDENCY RELATIONSHIPS

The indigenous peoples of the Oriente have been subjected to outside influences for more than a century. During the rubber boom (approximately 1880 to 1914), some groups were uprooted and the population in large parts of the region was coerced into patron-peon relationships. This pattern was perpetuated and expanded after 1914 by a motley class of merchants trading in cinchona bark, tagua nuts (vegetable ivory), animal skins, gold and lumber. Some traditional agricultural estates and tea and sugar plantations, established in western Pastaza during the 1930s, equally relied on debt dependency, and often virtual slavery of indigenous labor. Further impacts came with oil exploration in Pastaza during the 1920s and 1940s. Finally, the war with Peru in 1941 displaced and divided ethnic groups by permanently blocking communication across the contentious boundary which resulted.

The most pervasive historical influence, however, was that of the missionaries. From the 1880s the Oriente was progressively divided among largely foreign staffed missionary orders of the Catholic church: Carmelites in Sucumbíos, Josephines in Napo, Capuchins in Sucumbíos and Napo, and Dominicans in Pastaza.

The missionaries established a benevolent paternalistic relationship. Boarding schools, which are still landmarks in the main towns of the Oriente, were their main instruments in introducing "white civilization". The missionaries encouraged their charges to abandon their internecine conflicts, to change from a dispersed habitat to nucleated settlements, to adopt agriculture, and to integrate into the capitalist economy. New dress codes were introduced from the beginning, as shown in a fascinating collection of photos from the period 1880-1945 (Chiriboga y Cruz 1992).

The impact of the Catholic missions was most strongly felt among the Quichua (and the Shuar in the southern Oriente). From 1953, the Protestant Summer Institute of Linguistics (SIL) targeted the more isolated groups, notably the Huaorani, the Siona-Siecoya and the Cofan. These evangelists often worked closely with oil companies to further their mutual objectives (Colby and Dennet 1995).

After 1967 the disruptive influences increased significantly, in large part due to the discovery of oil. Texaco initiated oil development near Lago Agrio. Eventually several other foreign companies and Petroecuador became involved in large parts of Sucumbíos and Napo provinces. Many indigenous men were introduced to temporary wage labor, prostitution and consumer goods during the oil exploration phase. Women would often live in fear of the abusive practices of the oil workers. The routine dumping of toxic formation water and frequent oil spills into the rivers on which indigenous communities depend, by contrast, tended to increase indigenous environmental awareness and militancy. Generally, the oil companies have tried to make the *indígenas* dependent and cooperative through offers of gifts, community facilities and employment. This manipulation, which is excellently captured in Kane's (1995) portrait of the Huaorani case, often led to conflict within indigenous communities and organizations. While the environmental practices and community relations of the oil companies have somewhat improved over time, the manipulation of indigenous communities continues. In one case (see chapter VIII, "Santa Elena"), an oil company is even financing a CBE complex.

The flood of settlers which followed the new, oil-financed road network affected the *indígenas* in several ways. First, it displaced them from some of the best and most accessible agricultural soils. Second, it reduced the territory available for hunting and gathering. Finally, the example of the settlers and government policy encouraged the indigenous people to increase their reliance on agriculture and lumber extraction and to covet land as private property rather than a communal resource.

The resource base of the indigenous nations was further restricted when the government established nature reserves. Generally, the supporters of nature reserves, which include the government agency INEFAN, international and national NGOs, US and German aid agencies, and sectors of the ecotourism industry, were more concerned with environmental protection than the indigenous land rights. As a consequence, the indige-

nous nations were inadequately consulted and continue to consider the government-designated nature reserves as their own
reserves. With time, the proponents of nature reserves have
become more willing to incorporate an indigenous role in these
areas on condition that it conforms to their conservation objectives.

The impact of the conventional ecotourism industry, which
includes jungle lodges, foreign and Quito-based tour operators,
and local guides has been an additional concern for the indigenous peoples. A description of this industry is available in other
sources (Drumm 1991, Lemky 1992, Wesche et al. 1995, Pearson
and Middleton 1997, Rachowiecki 1997, Veltri 1998). Tourism
entrepreneurs often employ *indígenas* as native guides, boatmen,
and unqualified support staff, and visit indigenous territory and
settlements as part of their programs. Generally, the economic
benefits for indigenous communities have been limited and
unpredictable as entrepreneurs change priorities and destinations. The beneficiaries tended to be individuals employed by or
making deals with the tourism industry, a phenomenon which
contributed to social stratification and dissent within communities. Also, visits by tourist groups were often intrusive and uncontrolled.

INDIGENOUS STRATEGIES TOWARD SELF RELIANCE

In the past, the indigenous peoples have reacted to the challenges outlined above in an uncoordinated fashion, combining acceptance, submission, passive resistance, retreat, and only occasionally, active resistance. In recent years, however, a more proactive and coordinated strategy toward self reliant development has started to emerge. Key components of this strategy are political organization, land rights, cultural survival, conservation, and community based ecotourism.

Political Organization: The first important step was the formation of organizations and federations which united communities of the same language group. The Shuar (since 1964) and the Quichua (since 1969), the most populous groups, were the first to be impacted and became the most acculturated. They in turn initiated the process of community and political organization and have played a leadership role ever since. By 1990, all of the smaller nationalities had formed their own organizations. The federations are affiliates of CONFENIAE, CONAIE and the Quito-based international organization COICA. These higher order organizations have fostered self-reliant development by establishing and implementing indigenous policies. They have also served in representing indigenous interests in relation to government and to Amazon frontier interest groups such as oil companies and settlers. The political evolution has led to the formation of the Pachacutik movement which has successfully presented indigenous candidates for election to the national congress in Quito. One of their early achievements was the creation of CON-PLADEIN (National Council for the Planning and Development of Indigenous and Negro Peoples) with offices in the Presidency of the Republic. This organization is strengthening the regional bodies and directing development initiatives to indigenous and Afro-ecuadorian areas.

Land Rights: The foremost objective of the indigenous organizations has been to protect and legalize indigenous lands in the face of encroachment by settlers, government-designated protected areas and oil companies. They have pursued this objective with increasing militancy, with tactics including strategic colonization of unoccupied'areas and a march of thousands from Puyo to Quito, led by OPIP in 1992. As a result, more than one third of the Oriente is now recognized or legalized as indigenous territory. The push for expansion of indigenous land rights continues in ambiguously defined areas and in government-designated protected areas.

The core of the struggle for land rights has been the concept of communal property. Communal territory is seen as the foundation of the survival of the community in harmony with its ancestral environment. By contrast, most indigenous organizations believe that private land property facilitates the maximization of individual gain, at the expense of the community, while encouraging resource exploitation and social stratification. Furthermore, it is seen as leading to the eventual polarization of land ownership and the sale of indigenous lands to non-indigenous landowners.

Cultural Survival: Closely interrelated with the protection of the indigenous land base has been the objective of protecting the cultural heritage. Indigenous organizations have demanded that the Ecuadorian constitution recognize Ecuador as a pluri-national, pluri-cultural state in which indigenous communities should have special rights as "different" citizens (Ruiz 1993). A number of efforts have been made to maintain and protect bilingual education, community cohesion, indigenous environmental practices and knowledge, handicrafts and mythology.

This by no means implies an attempt to revert to the stage of isolated subsistence societies. A century of change under Western influences precludes this, and such a project would be unacceptable to most of the indigenous population. Rather, the objective of indigenous organizations is the harmonization of the protection and evolution of indigenous traditions with controlled, selective integration into the national and global society and economy.

Conservation: An important instrument of indigenous organizations to further both the quest for a communal territorial base and cultural survival, is a renewed commitment to environmental conservation. In 1988 COICA issued a declaration to environmentalists and donor agencies which asserts that indigenous peoples with their "accumulated knowledge", "models of living" and "reverence and respect for the tropical forest and its other inhabitants ... are the keys to guaranteeing the future of the Amazon Basin." The declaration concludes that "the most effective defense of the Amazonian biosphere is the recognition of our ownership rights over our territories and the promotion of our models of living" (COICA 1989). CONFENIAE and its member organizations have taken up the principles of the COICA declaration in their claim to serve as guardians of the Ecuadorian Amazon, not only in their recognized territories but also in nature reserves set aside by the government.

Redford and Stearman (1993) and many other conservationists have disagreed with the COICA declaration, and argued the need for nature reserves which exclude indigenous peoples, on two grounds. First, they assert that the indigenous notion of conservation implies sustainable use and thus differs from the notion of Western conservationists which implies preservation in a natural state. Second, the critics claim that traditional indigenous uses were sometimes practiced unsustainably, and that indigenous groups have increasingly adopted the exploitative practices of the settlers in recent decades. Both of these critiques are doubtless justified to some extent. The critiques overlook, however, that the COICA declaration is not only intended as a statement of past practice but also represents a new policy commitment to conservation.

This commitment to conservation is strategic in several ways. First, it seeks to combat the erosion of native environmental traditions, and the trend toward the privatization and unsustainable exploitation of indigenous land. In essence, a renewed commitment to conservation is required to forestall the eventual collapse of indigenous society. Second, the conservation commitment justifies large land claims which are predicated on low intensity, sustainable resource use. Third, it supports the indigenous demand to play a role in the use and protection of government-decreed nature reserves. Finally, it is the basis for obtaining cooperation from environmental and developmental organizations. To obtain such cooperation, indigenous leaders have shown an increased willingness to find a compromise between their concept of conservation as sustainable use and the Western concept of preservation which excludes traditional types of indigenous use.

Though some indigenous communities continue to expand their commercial resource exploitation, there is increasing evidence of conservation practice. In several cases indigenous organizations have stopped or delayed oil development, or played a role in obliging oil companies to respect environmental regulations. Some communities have negotiated resource use rights in nature reserves in return for a commitment to play a role in nature reserve conservation. Others have imposed land clearing restrictions on their members or redefined their reserves for conservation purposes. Perhaps the most ambitious indigenous conservation project is the proposal by OPIP to convert the huge territory which it controls into an internationally recognized Indigenous Biosphere Reserve (Cerda 1998). These conservation measures are closely linked to the growing indigenous interest in ecotourism.

Community Based Ecotourism: Community based ecotourism is a recent addition to the indigenous strategy toward self reliance. It initially arose as a reaction to the encroachment of the mainstream ecotourism industry. The indigenous peoples hope that by assuming control of ecotourism in their territories, they can capture a larger and more predictable share of the tourist dollar, and limit the negative social and cultural impacts of tourist visits. With time a broader appreciation of the advantages of CBE has developed. This led to the adoption of CBE as part of the general strategy towards self reliance (COICA-CONFENIAE 1993) and its rapid spread during the last five years.

The advantages of CBE as a development option are outlined below:

1. If properly managed, CBE is a viable commercial development option which is environmentally sustainable; a small number of tourists per year can provide a higher income than more destructive alternatives such as agriculture and lumber extraction. These alternatives are particularly precarious since indigenous communities typically occupy poor soils and remote locations. The remoteness of many CBE communities, while an obstacle to other types of commercial resource use, is part of their

attraction for ecotourists. Furthermore, the transportation and communication facilities which are set up for tourists also facilitate access to urban centers for the community as a whole.

An additional advantage is the compatibility with other small scale economic activities practiced in the communities. Tourists are attracted in part by the possibility to learn about traditional indigenous resource use practices and generally do not perceive small scale sustainable resource use as conflicting with ecotourism. Tourists also constitute a market for locally produced food, handicrafts and, potentially, medicinal products. Local materials can largely be used to build the tourist *cabaña* complexes. Thus ecotourism can contribute to the diversification of economic activities within the communities.

2. CBE helps to advance indigenous land rights and environmental alliances as illustrated by the case of the Cuyabeno Defense Comittee (Drumm 1993). Ecotourism, as a recognized commercial enterprise, provides an economic justification for the allocation of large communal territories to indigenous communities. This is important politically since there have been strong pressures in Ecuador to divide up areas considered "unused" and "unproductive" for allocation to users who would make them "productive".

The commitment to ecotourism is also tangible evidence of the indigenous commitment to conservation, which strengthens indigenous demands to be recognized as defenders of the Amazon and to play a role in the management and use of government-declared nature reserves. Aid organizations and environmental NGOs have discovered CBE as an instrument for their conservation objectives and have given it considerable support. Within individual indigenous communities, ecotourism has strengthened the arguments for protection of communal reserves against the pressures toward private land ownership.

3. Finally, CBE can contribute to the strengthening of indigenous culture and pride. CBE generally seeks to market indigenous environmental knowledge and symbiotic relations with the rainforest, not as a quaint relic but as an alternative to destructive Western ways. This provides an incentive for the recuperation of traditional knowledge and practices and a renewed respect for the wisdom of the elders, who are asked to play a role in transmitting traditional knowledge.

Such positive elements are, of course, potentially counterbalanced by the threat of negative visitor influences. The purpose of CBE is precisely to minimize such negative influences while maximizing benefits to the community by limiting visitor numbers and obtaining a fair price. If tourists are engaged in a harmonious intercultural exchange, this may eventually elicit a long-term commitment on the part of the traveler to support survival of the indigenous way of life and even to adopt some of its precepts.

V
CHARACTERISTICS OF COMMUNITY BASED ECOTOURISM

While CBE is an alternative to and distinct from the ecotourism practiced by non-indigenous lodges, tour companies and guides, it is difficult to quantify this distinction. As a minimum, the CBE concept implies that the ecotourism activity is based in community territory, that the community as a whole or its members have substantial control and involvement, that a major proportion of the benefits remain in the community, and that the project has been approved by the elected representatives of the community and of the relevant higher order organization. These criteria determined the selection of enterprises for inclusion in this guidebook. A number of enterprises involving indigenous owners and operators which did not meet the above criteria were excluded.

TYPES OF CBE ENTERPRISES

Three main types of CBE enterprises can be distinguished. The purest model, which is generally favored by the indigenous federations, is the community owned and managed enterprise. This model has been practiced by RICANCIE (Network of Indigenous Communities of the Upper Napo for Intercultural Exchange and Ecotourism, see Chapter IX). It seeks to spread income to all community members by employing them in tourist services using a rotation system. Remaining profits are allocated to community projects.

While this approach is the most egalitarian, it is also the most difficult to implement and maintain. In most communities the degree of members' interest in tourism and their willingness to contribute labor on a consistent basis varies. Though traditions of sharing and communal labor exist, the notion of a long-term communal enterprise requiring the permanent, consistent commitment of all community members has to be learned and reinforced through positive experience if it can be achieved at all in the long-term. Community solidarity is particularly difficult to maintain if the communal labor investment in the building of *cabañas* and other infrastructure does not produce income in the short term and when promised employment does not materialize. Once a predictable flow of income has been established, it may be easier to rally most community members around such an enterprise.

Additional problems with the communal enterprise approach are the complexity and slowness of democratic decision-making and the inconsistent quality of services, which results from the widely spread involvement of poorly trained community members. As a result, the community enterprise model is in the process of being adapted toward a more centralized administration, with the allocation of responsibilities being mainly to specialized, trained community members and the restriction of membership to those who are truly committed to the ecotourism enterprise.

The second, increasingly common type of CBE involves family or group initiatives within communities. This is a more flexible type, since it is based on voluntary participation and arrangements between individuals can be more easily adjusted to changing demand. Community benefits are still relatively high, since labor and services will be contracted within the group.

Other community members may also benefit through the sale of handicrafts.

Joint ventures between an indigenous community, federation, or family and a non-indigenous partner represent the third and least frequent type. Two distinct kinds of joint venture agreements can be distinguished. In the first, the non-indigenous partner supplies the tourists, transportation to the community, and, where required, a multilingual guide. The indigenous partner, in turn, takes care of the program and arrangements within the community. In the second case, the non-indigenous partner obtains a long-term lease in the community territory, builds and manages the tourist complex, and in return guarantees employment and other specified benefits for the community.

Though indigenous communities generally prefer to be fully self reliant in their tourism business, they face obstacles in becoming so. Especially in the early stages, they lack the knowledge and resources to directly access the international market which supplies most of the ecotourists. Even in the local urban centers, CBE enterprises generally have difficulty competing with the more astute and manipulative non-indigenous guides for the backpacker clientele. Furthermore, affluent tourists frequently require the assurance of dealing with established operators which can guarantee quality and provide specialized guides with the appropriate language skills. These considerations have encouraged joint ventures in some cases and informal arrangements with non-indigenous operators in others.

Any one of the three basic types of CBE outlined above may be appropriate, depending on the stage of tourism development and the particular circumstances of the community concerned. Thus no value judgment regarding the different types of CBE enterprises is attempted. All current enterprises which are based in communities, have significant community control and involvement, provide important benefits for the community, and have the support of the elected representatives are included in this book. Equally, the book lists those responsible tourism operators which were identified by CBE enterprises as their established links to the market. CBE tourists wishing to receive the organizational and language services of more sophisticated, Western style tourism operators should deal through the operators listed.

QUALITY AND STYLE
OF THE TOURISM EXPERIENCE

CBE provides a travel experience which differs from that offered by non-indigenous operators. In all CBE cases described, the community has made a conscious choice in favor of CBE. Thus the tourist feels like a welcome guest rather than an interloper in the community. While the tourist *cabañas* are normally set apart from the settlement, there is the opportunity to casually interact with the host community and to observe the daily cycle of life in a relaxed atmosphere.

Visitors will have the chance to both learn about indigenous subsistence uses of the local environment and to experience the beauty of the surrounding natural ecosystem. The program normally includes spontaneous or organized contact with the local culture, including current practices and long-standing traditions. Generally the program is unhurried, with adjustments made depending on weather and other circumstances.

The level of services provided varies from community to community, reflecting different exposure to Western influences, extent of previous contact with tourists, and quality of local leadership. Most CBE enterprises are unsophisticated, reflecting the fact that CBE is recent and that the indigenous hosts are only starting to learn about the requirements and expectations of Western tourists. It is this very lack of sophistication, and the sincere, occasionally awkward efforts of the indigenous hosts to learn and to please which will strike any sensitive tourist.

Indigenous guides are typically modest and quiet, exhibiting little of the macho bravado which characterizes some of their non-indigenous colleagues. Female tourists in particular generally appreciate this distinction. Many guides have received some formal training and are certified as "native guides" by CETUR, the Ecuadorian Tourism Corporation. They have a basic awareness of the needs and interests of foreign tourists. Language is a constraint, since most indigenous guides only speak their native language and Spanish.

Lodging and eating facilities are simple, except in the cases of a few joint venture enterprises. Nevertheless, they meet the basic requirements of reasonably adaptable adventurous travelers. All *cabaña* complexes are built from local materials. Beds generally have adequate mattresses, clean sheets and mosquito netting. Basic standards of hygiene are observed with regard to food and water. The cuisine is generally unsophisticated, incorporating purchased as well as community-produced foods.

A major problem for CBE communities is access to and communication with the market. This book is a tool to overcome part of this problem. Most CBE communities lack modern means of communication. In many cases, information must be relayed by messenger. Even the organized networks of CBE communities with offices in the local urban centers have only rudimentary means of communication, experience frequent technical failures and often keep somewhat irregular office hours. In view of their isolation, many CBE communities also need a bit of lead time to prepare themselves for the visitors' arrival. Thus making arrangements for a CBE visit is often a challenge for tourists used to Western convenience and predictability.

Nevertheless, in most cases CBE visits can be arranged in Spanish by mail, fax or phone and (in the near future) by e-mail with sufficient lead time or within a day or two of the tourist's arrival in one of the staging centers, i.e. Lago Agrio, Coca, Tena or Puyo. In each of these centers, a sufficient variety of CBE offerings is available so that the time-constrained tourist is assured of a quick arrangement. This may not necessarily be the case, though, for the more remote locations, and it is especially here where responsible private sector partners of CBE play an important role.

Quichua pottery
(K. Bemben)

VI
THE ROLE OF THE
RESPONSIBLE TRAVELER

Before setting out for the Oriente and engaging in CBE, the visitor should reflect on the meaning and implications of community based ecotourism. CBE is a fragile experiment in which indigenous people seek to strengthen their precarious existence by combining tourism income with the conservation of their culture and their environment. THE QUEST OF THE RESPONSIBLE TRAVELER SHOULD BE TO LEARN, TO BE UNDERSTANDING, TO SHARE, TO CONTRIBUTE - RATHER THAN TO ACT AS A CONSUMER WHO SEEKS MAXIMUM GRATIFICATION AT MINIMUM EXPENSE.

Responsible travelers should be willing to accept the different priorities, ways and standards of their indigenous hosts. Since their hosts are new to the ecotourism "business", a few rough edges have to be expected. Also, travelers must keep in mind that CBE has the purpose of benefiting and involving the community at large. Thus, CBE necessarily has an operating style which differs from that of a capitalist enterprise, which normally seeks to maximize efficiency and private profit without regard for the social consequences.

The following guidelines should help to make your visit of a CBE community a constructive and rewarding experience:

Respect for Local Customs: Be aware of your actions and appearance, and how they may be perceived by your hosts. Learn about the customs of your host community and don't judge your hosts based on your own cultural background - perceptions of punctuality, manners, formality, etc. often vary. Follow guidelines given by your hosts; if in doubt ask your guide. Dress conservatively. Recognize that you are much richer than your hosts; don't show off your affluence.

Economic Contribution: Be aware of the social consequences of your travel choices. Dealing directly with CBE enterprises assures maximum retention and spread of income. Realize that private operators may underbid CBE enterprises by cutting corners and reducing benefits to others. If you choose tour companies, consider the responsible operators listed in this book or inquire what proportion of your payment your host community receives. Consider visiting communities which receive few visitors!

Pay your hosts a fair price. Buy handicrafts in the community. Consider a donation for community projects. When making a gift, do so to the elected authorities in view of other community members, to assure its use for the intended purpose.

Environmental Practice: Lead by example. Do not leave trash, and pick up the trash of others. Stay on trails and do not disturb wildlife. If you observe poor environmental practices among your hosts or fellow travelers, politely suggest improvements. Recognize that your hosts belong to hunting societies which continue to rely on protein from the forest while they are diversifying into ecotourism and reducing their need for hunting. Thus do not impose purist, urban-based preservation standards on your hosts. If you observe hunting for purely commercial purposes, however, feel free to discuss your views. You should avoid buying handicrafts made from bird feathers and animal teeth to discourage commercial hunting.

Respect for Privacy: Most indigenous people are shy and appreciate privacy. Do not intrude into homes or the private gardens immediately surrounding them without asking permission or unless invited. Ask before taking photos of people. Avoid sexual contact; avoid nudity and intimate displays of affection in public.

Preparation: Before heading for the Oriente, try to improve your Spanish and consider some readings from the bibliography provided in this book.

Networking: When returning home, assume the role of ambassador for CBE. Your indigenous friends rely on people like you to expand their network of contacts!

VII
COMMUNITY BASED
ECOTOURISM IN SUCUMBÍOS

Sucumbíos province (Maps 2,3), which roughly corresponds to the Río Aguarico watershed, is a multiethnic region. Its indigenous people include the Quichua, Cofan, Siona, Siecoya and Shuar. It ranges from the Andes to the lowland Peruvian boundary, with a large part of its western mountains included in the Cayambe-Coca Ecological Reserve, while the bulk of its eastern lowlands is covered by the Cuyabeno Wildlife Reserve.

Between these two reserves lies the most heavily oil and settler impacted area of the Oriente. The bustling but unappealing oil town of Lago Agrio is the center of this area and contains most services which tourists require. It is also the most important transportation hub of the Oriente with roads to Quito, Shushufindi Coca, and the Colombian border. To the east and southeast, roads connect with the Río Cuyabeno (at the Lago Agrio-Puerto el Carmen de Putumayo road bridge of the Río Cuyabeno), and the Río Aguarico at Chiritza and Poza Honda (the latter east of Shushufindi). These rivers give access to most of the province's CBE projects.

The two nature reserves of the area are strikingly different. The Cayambe-Coca Reserve is rugged and mainly of interest to adventurous hikers. It has spectacular topography including two volcanoes, the Cayambe and the Reventador, and ranges from ice and snow on the Cayambe to the lower montane forest.

The Cuyabeno Wildlife Reserve, by contrast, is largely flat, with the greatest concentration of lagoons in the Oriente. These are its main attractions, since they offer a fascinating interplay between lagoon and seasonally flooded forest with an extraordinary concentration of aquatic and terrestrial fauna.

Indigenous territories and the western part of the Cuyabeno Reserve were heavily impacted by oil and settlers. In the central part of the province, the indigenous population was almost completely displaced, except for the Cofan Reserve of Dureno which forms an island in a sea of settlers. In the west, the Quichua have managed to hold on to a belt of territory abutting on the Sumaco-Galeras Park. In the east, the Siona, Siecoya, Cofan and Quichua hold an even more strategic position, buffering the whole southern side of the Cuyabeno Reserve. Furthermore, some communities negotiated land rights within the Reserve (Map 3) which have turned the *indígenas* into veritable park guardians.

This strategic position near or in nature reserves has encouraged CBE development by communities of all the language groups of the area except the Shuar. A broad variety of CBE programs are available and tourists may consider using the region's multiethnicity to their advantage by visiting CBE projects of several language groups.

SIONATOUR

SIONATOUR is the ecotourism agency of the Siona organization ONISE. It was founded in 1996 with the help of FEPP
(Fundación Ecuatoriana Populorum Progresio). Its aim is to support the three Siona communities -Biaña, Orahuëayá and Puerto
Bolívar - in their community based ecotourism development.
SIONATOUR replaced Biosisituris in 1998 and a stronger commitment to community control resulted. Biaña is a community
enterprise, while conflict between community enterprise and private enterprise continues in Orahuëayá. Puerto Bolívar offers
exclusively private enterprise tourism, but tours booked through
SIONATOUR will certainly help its evolution toward CBE. To
inquire about tours to these communities, contact

> SIONATOUR (FEPP)
> 12 de Febrero 267 y 10 de Agosto
> Lago Agrio, Sucumbíos
> Tel: (06) 831 875, fax: (06)830 232
> or by mail at:
> SIONATOUR (FEPP) - Lago Agrio,
> Casilla 17 110 5202
> Quito, Ecuador

Highlights of the three individual Siona communities are
provided in the following descriptions.
Prices: $40 to $60/person/day depending on group size
and duration of program

ORAHUËAYÁ (SIONATOUR)

This community is set in an astonishingly pristine environment adjacent to an area heavily impacted by colonization and oil development. This contrast can be readily observed on the trip from Lago Agrio to Orahuëayá, which is located on the Río Shushufindi. Its easy accessibility, quality lodgings, and picturesque natural attractions make this community an ideal destination for the average hiker who seeks a range of versatile activities.

The ecotourism complex is located on a bluff overlooking the river, three hours southeast of Lago Agrio by road and a further two hours by canoe. The 15 families of the Orahuëayá community are dispersed with no clear locational center. The tourism facilities are situated far from community houses, providing a feeling of seclusion.

The infrastructure consists of one well-kept, fully equipped sleeping *cabaña* which accommodates up to nine people, a separate kitchen *cabaña* with dining room, and a third *cabaña* used for cultural presentations. Washroom facilities consist of two flush toilets and two showers, located down a lengthy flight of wooden stairs. There also exists a second sleeping *cabaña* for larger groups that is shared with the community of Biaña. Its use is coordinated through SIONATOUR.

In the future, Orahuëayá plans to further develop its own complex by adding a small museum of cultural artifacts. Additionally, informative sessions for tourists, including detailed demonstrations of the construction of traditional Siona homes and residences, are being organized. Community members are shy but very friendly and welcoming to tourists. They enjoy having their pictures taken!

Partaking in Orahuëayá's CBE program allows visitors to become aware of the culture and values of the Siona people. The atmosphere is relaxed and allows tourists to enjoy the surroundings at their own pace. Typical visits last four days with the option of shortening or extending the program. The presence and participation of the community *shaman* in most of the activities makes for a more authentic experience. Tourist activities include a presentation by the *shaman* on the history of the Siona people, fishing on the Río Shushufindi, a four-hour jungle hike and a canoe ride to a still-water lagoon located just off the main river. As a nocturnal event, the guide escorts tourists by dugout paddle canoe to the Río Shushufindi for caiman watching. During hours of free time, tourists can engage in activities such as jungle trekking, swimming, and birdwatching.

The ecotourism program is run in a rotational pattern by various members of the community who manage the cooking, guiding, canoeing, and cultural presentations. There are two guides available, Cesario Yiyocuro and Leonardo Payaguaje, who have not had any official training, yet are extremely knowledgeable about flora and fauna. Any specific requests or needs can be easily accommodated as the guides are very flexible, friendly and open to questions.

It is important for tourists to note that the only CBE program in Orahuëayá is run in conjunction with SIONATOUR. The community requests a minimum of two visitors and can accommodate up to nine people. Make arrangements in advance.

BIAÑA (SIONATOUR)

Biaña, which signifies "River of Birds" in Siona, is a tranquil little community along the southern banks of the Río Aguarico, where one can take part in leisurely programs in the company of enthusiastic guides. Whether discovering the secrets of the rainforest on a casual walk or paddling down nearby serene rivers, each activity complements the rich natural and cultural history of the Siona people. The atmosphere is effortless and relaxed, the food is delectable and there is much to be contemplated and experienced in this small green paradise.

Upriver and downriver from Biaña are the port of Poza Honda and the community of San Pablo de Kantesiya, respectively. The tourist *cabañas* are located in a clearing 25 m off the shores of the Río Aguarico and complement the dispersed settlement pattern of the community. The surrounding area comprises a web of trails and small rivers which are a haven for naturalists and birders. Most activities are a short distance from the *cabañas* and are reachable by canoe. This means that you will pass by the communities of San Pablo de Kantesiya and some of Biaña's farms during your excursions. If you ask ahead of time you should be able to stop at any one of these places for a visit.

This community-owned and operated project has gradually evolved since its creation in 1994 with the help of ONISE and SIONATOUR. The project is staffed on a rotational basis by several members of the community who participate in the various tasks of cooking, motoring, guiding and cleaning. There are three trained guides in total. Lisandro Piaguaje is the most experienced guide as well as tourism coordinator and will go to great lengths to meet the visitor's requests. The other guides are Federico and Santo Piaguaje.

Tourism infrastructure consists of two comfortable *cabañas*, built of pambil and palm tree leaves in traditional Siona design. One serves as a sleeping *cabaña* and can accommodate up to eight tourists. It is equipped with mattresses, sheets, pillows and mosquito nets. The other serves as a kitchen/dining lounge. The tourist site also has toilets and showers, with clean running water that is manually pumped from a cement well.

The tourist program is very flexible; there are fixed activities, but they can be arranged to suit your particular needs. Your best bet is to discuss it with your guide upon arrival or even during your visit. You will have the opportunity to take a four to five-hour walk through the jungle, where your guide will explain the uses of medicinal plants, show you a giant leaf-cutter ant colony and call on jungle creatures using mysterious devices! Canoeing up a beautiful and meandering tributary of the Río Aguarico is also a highlight as it is a great location for swimming. One should, however, avoid the small dugout canoes *(quillas)* available on the Río Aguarico, since the strong current makes their use dangerous for all but the most experienced paddlers. You can go fishing for piranha and catfish in the Río Shushufindi and if the season is right, go caiman watching at night. Also included is a candlelight tale of the history of Biaña shamanism and a colorful cultural presentation with native dances. During this presentation, you will have the chance to drink *chicha*, learn to weave *cernidoras* (used to sift flour and rice) and buy crafts.

The community hopes to expand their tourism attractions in the near future. Tentative plans include an overnight jungle trek, a two-hour hike along the river and the construction of a second *cabaña* on the nearby Río Aguas Negras.

Accessing Biaña is relatively simple. Leaving from Lago Agrio, you catch an early ride either by bus or *ranchera* to the port of Chiritza. Here, your guides will greet you and take you down the Río Aguarico for a 45-minute canoe ride to the community.

Spontaneous arrivals are not advisable as the community needs time to prepare for tourists. Although it is possible for as few as two visitors to enter the community, it is preferable to come as a larger group. This is profitable for both the community and the tourist since prices tend to diminish with increasing group size.

All in all, the secret to enjoying Biaña is knowing how to relax. If you are the kind of tourist who can appreciate a slower pace of living and is not in a rush to discover everything at once, then let Biaña be your own private haven for a couple of days.

PUERTO BOLÍVAR (SIONATOUR)

In the heart of the Cuyabeno Reserve lies a network of scenic freshwater lagoons. The picturesque landscape created by these alluring water bodies is constantly in flux due to drastic changes in water levels. The area is characterized by unique fauna such as the prehistoric Hoatzin bird, the manatee, and the pink freshwater dolphin. Tourist programs in the area are centered in Laguna Grande, the largest of the chain. They typically combine exploration of the natural setting with a short canoe trip downstream to the Siona community of Puerto Bolívar. Although the tourism ventures run by members of this community do not presently meet the criteria of community based ecotourism, Puerto Bolívar has been included in the book due to its unique set of natural attractions and its connection with SIONATOUR (which seeks to promote CBE). It is hoped that this relationship will lead to the development of a community based project.

The lagoons are easily accessed by motorized canoe from the Cuyabeno River Bridge (Puente Cuyabeno), three hours by road east of Lago Agrio. The small center of Puerto Bolívar is ideally located slightly downriver from the Laguna Grande, allowing for combined nature-culture tourism programs. The traditional spatial organization of the Siona culture has influenced the dispersal of its population, with small agricultural plots along the Río Cuyabeno. The river and settlement surroundings are enhanced by spectacular tropical forest vegetation.

Some 30 years ago, the Siona of this area became involved in tourism. Only recently have they begun to break out of the service-oriented employment they have been providing for tour agencies in the area. Seven community members of Puerto

Bolívar have individually set up their own privately-run *cabañas* of which three are on Laguna Grande and four are spaced at intervals along the Río Cuyabeno between the lagoons and the community itself. (The owners of these facilities have collectively agreed to charge incoming tour groups fixed prices). At present these family-run enterprises do not benefit the community directly; however, it is hoped that future developments will lead towards increased communal management of incoming tourists.

There also exists a *cabaña* complex called "La Hormiga", located on Laguna Grande, which is presently under the administration of INEFAN. In the past, the Siona of Puerto Bolívar were involved in the administration of this operation, but as the management is currently undergoing structural reorganization, it is difficult to predict if it will return to a community based venture, or whether eventual communal profits will be collected.

Programs based in or near the lagoons generally consist of piranha fishing, caiman and bird watching, jungle walks, swimming and paddling in dugout canoes. An important consideration is the extremely limited boat access to the reservoirs between December and February due to low water levels. During this time it is possible to explore by foot - surely walking through the lagoon beds provides a much different experience than traveling by canoe!

To reach the Puerto Bolívar area, one must travel to the Puente Cuyabeno, at kilometer 100 of the Lago Agrio-Tipishca road. From there, a scenic two and a half-hour canoe ride down the winding, mystical Río Cuyabeno brings you to Laguna Grande. An additional hour brings you to Puerto Bolívar. The average group size visiting this area is between five and seven persons and tours typically last about four days. Be ready to pay the Reserve entrance fee at the INEFAN office upon arrival at the

Puente Cuyabeno ($10 for foreigners and $1 for nationals and residents). Since access into the area is regulated by INEFAN, spontaneous arrivals are not permitted. In order to support the best approximation of CBE in the Cuyabeno Lagoons area, travel arrangements should be made through SIONATOUR.

Quichua pottery
(K. Bemben)

COMUNA COFAN DURENO

Comuna Cofan Dureno, opposite the settler town of Dureno on the south shore of the Río Aguarico, offers an authentic jungle experience only an hour's drive east of Lago Agrio. A difficult two-hour hike from the community is then required to reach the tourist *cabañas* near a small lagoon and the Río Pisuri. A variety of activities can be enjoyed at a leisurely pace with the friendly and informal guides. The Cofan people display a strong cultural pride and are eager to share their traditional way of life with the ecotourist.

Although surrounded by settlers, the territory covers 9 500 hectares of largely untouched forest. The 300 community members occupy small plots of land along the Río Aguarico where maize, *plátano, yuca,* and coffee are grown. These are partly sold at the weekly markets of Lago Agrio and Dureno, on the north shore.

This CBE project is a cooperative effort that was initiated in 1989 by four active community members. They donated their time to build two cabañas which can house up to seven people, a latrine and a dugout paddle canoe. All four equally share the tasks of cooking, cleaning, paddling and guiding. The community takes part by hosting tourists during afternoon visits to local families where handicrafts may be purchased.

Due to a lack of marketing, only 15 tourists have visited the *cabañas* since they were built ten years ago. This by no means diminishes the quality and coordination of the program. The four-day adventure begins when you are met on the north shore of the Río Aguarico by small dugout canoe *(quilla)* and poled across to the Cofan territory. From there, a demanding two-hour hike through primary forest brings you to a basic sleeping *cabaña* with only a platform and thatched roof. On the second day, prepare for a day-long guided hike to an ideal spot for observing Squirrel monkeys in their natural habitat. The next day, consider replacing your regular cup of coffee with an early morning swing on a liana (tarzan style). Later on, relax along the Río Pisuri, for a peaceful afternoon of fishing. On the final day, you will hike back to the shore of the Río Aguarico, tour the community and purchase handicrafts. Cultural tidbits are randomly inserted into the program and may include such things as basket weaving, house construction, and demonstrations of medicinal and edible plants. Evenings are always a special time for storytelling and recounting local legends.

It is a bit difficult to advise the community of your arrival or desire to visit, but this should not deter you in any way. For the flexible and resourceful traveler, Comuna Cofan Dureno is easily accessible. Take a bus to the settler town of Dureno (Putumayo or Petrolera transport companies) and from there make arrangements to cross the Río Aguarico. Three days notice is appreciated in order for food and supplies to be purchased and to arrange a meeting time with your guide. This is not always possible since the community is difficult to contact. To arrange for a visit to Comuna Cofan Dureno, approach any Cofan community member at the Saturday and Sunday markets either in Lago Agrio or Dureno. Ask about the ecotourism program and mention the guides' names: Laureano Quenema, Delfin Criollo, Lino Mendua or Hector Quenema. It is also possible to contact someone in the communal Cofan house at the bridge in the colonist town of Dureno, for help crossing to the south shore. A mosquito net, a ground sheet, a light sleeping bag, a rain poncho and rubber boots are essential as no equipment is provided by the community. Remember to pack lightly because you are responsible for carrying it all in!

Price: $35/person/day (groups of 1 to 3), $30/person/day (groups of 4 to 7), $1/person entrance fee.

Contact: Frente de la Defensa de la Amazonía, Eloy Alfaro no. 352 y Av. Colombia, Lago Agrio, Sucumbíos, telefax: (06) 831 930, e-mail: Admin@FDA. ecuanex.net.ec

SINANGÜÉ

The adventurous traveler visiting this Cofan community has the opportunity to experience exceptional scenery and wildlife within a cool, high-altitude jungle environment. Sinangüé is located in the foothills of the Andes, along the Río Aguarico, in the northeastern part of the Cayambe-Coca Ecological Reserve. This area was largely remote and untouched until recently, when a new road was built passing within a kilometer of the Cofan territory. The community is hopeful that this road will facilitate greater access to its ecotourism program.

The Cofan have long inhabited this region, yet only a small number of families reside here today. Their territory extends into the hills from the right bank of the Río Aguarico. The majority of the homes are dispersed along the riverfront, apart from a small cluster which forms the community center. The tourism facilities are located here, along with a schoolhouse and an impressive thatched roof gazebo, which offers stunning vistas of the wide Aguarico below and the surrounding montane forests.

Visitors have the chance to experience Cofan lifestyle as they lodge in the center of the village and are under the watchful eye of inquisitive children. As of now, there is no cultural program, yet members have shown interest in preparing an hour of local music and dance and selling hand-made crafts. A community based program is underway and the president of the community, Victor Quenema, is expecting a fairly steady inflow of tourists, now that the new road provides easier access and reliable transportation.

Presently, meals are prepared and served by members of the community who wish to accommodate tourists in their homes. Sleeping arrangements are in the current president's house, where a room with two bunk beds and screened windows is available. A separate bathroom facility has two flushable toilets. There is also a large gazebo, a pleasant shaded spot to read and take in the impressive upwelling of cloud masses that build in the sky. Equipment such as mattresses, mosquito nets, lifejackets and paddle dugout canoes may continuously be available, but the tourist should verify this with the organizers ahead of time.

Two guides who are employed as INEFAN park guards are available for hikes. There is also the possibility of canoeing, swimming or playing soccer with the local children. There is one main trail that cuts through the territory, and hikes ranging from three to five hours can be arranged. Midway, this trail extends to a secluded part of the Río Cabeno, where a calm stretch of water cascades into an abrupt two–meter waterfall. These hikes are relatively simple and bands of Squirrel monkeys can frequently be spotted.

Sinangüe is located approximately 50 km northwest of the town of Lumbaqui, which is one and half hours west of Lago Agrio. It is reached by the new Interoceánica road along the Río Aguarico that will eventually connect this part of the Oriente to the Andean city of Tulcan. At present, only school buses run along this road, but in the near future, *rancheras* and inter-city buses will offer more reliable and frequent services. A $10 fee may be levied at the INEFAN gate.

Tourists have the option to either plan their visit ahead of time or simply arrive unannounced. Two weeks notice should be given to the Sinangüe park guards at the INEFAN station in Lago Agrio for prior arrangements. The community will be notified through them and plans will be made to meet tourists in Cabeno.

If you do not wish to confirm your visit in advance and are interested in a little challenge, you can make your own way to Siñangüé. To locate the trailhead to the community ask the driver to let you off at Cabeno and inquire around. The trail is not obvious from the road, so it would be in your best interest to find a local person to lead you through it with a machete. Although the community is within one kilometer of the road, it can be troublesome to reach as several small streams and the Río Aguarico must be traversed. The center of the community lies slightly downriver from the end of the trail. One could attempt to yell across for assistance; however, the river is very loud and may overpower your calls. Best strip down, swim across and humbly present yourself on the other side.

Price: $30 to $40/person/day, $1 community entrance fee.
Contact: INEFAN, Calle 10 de Agosto entre Manabi y Colombia, Lago Agrio, Sucumbíos

SIECOYA

Three hours downriver from Puerto Chiritza lies Siecoya (Map 3), home to a community-supported enterprise called Piraña Tour. This privately-run venture of César Piaguaje and Gilberto Piguaje is well organized and offers many attractions to a wide range of tourists. Visitors will be delighted with the exceptional cuisine, knowledgeable guides and their encounter with a powerful and wise *shaman.*

Piraña Tour operates from the large, open-sided Cabaña Piraña as well as the homes of César and his father Cesario, the local *shaman,* 15 minutes upriver from the center of Siecoya. Tourists are mainly lodged in the *cabaña,* but may also stay at César's or Cesario's home - within minutes of the *cabaña* - depending on the visitor's primary intent. The latter two are reserved for visitors (mainly researchers and students), who are involved in self-directed research projects relating to the ecology of the area or aspects of the Siecoya culture and customs.

Most tourists stay at the open-sided Cabaña Piraña complex, which contains a sleeping *cabaña,* a large room for eating and sitting, latrines, and an enclosed kitchen. Eventually, showers will be installed, so visitors will no longer be required to bathe in the Río Aguarico. Meals, whether in the field or at the *cabaña,* are of exceptional quality. César's 17-year old son José has a remarkable talent for preparing exquisite dishes with the simplest of ingredients.

Piraña Tour offers two basic programs. Those wishing to experience the jungle and the community without excessive physical demands should opt for the four-day program. Guests are welcomed in Lago Agrio and transported to the Cabaña Piraña, followed by a reception and information session. The following morning, they are taken bird watching and later attend sessions on Siecoya traditions and astrology, followed by a handicraft sale. Tourists are also led through the jungle to the "black" waters of the Río Pañayacu for piranha fishing, animal sighting and to learn Siecoya traditions (such as dart-making and palm bag weaving) in the rainforest. At times, the trail may be flooded, so be prepared to wade or swim because César does not stop for high waters! Leisure time can be spent swimming, meditating, or going on individual walks with the guides. The evening is dedicated to caiman watching by canoe.

Those who prefer a more challenging program should opt for the eight-day canoeing and hiking excursion. The terrain and overnight camping of the journey make this option more physically demanding than the four-day program. This trip involves sleeping under the stars in the easternmost part of the Cuyabeno Wildlife Reserve on the rich heritage grounds of the Siecoya people. Guests visit the Río Lagartococha along the Peruvian boundary, a veritable maze of unspoiled black water lagoons. Keep in mind that Piraña Tours´ tent only sleeps five, thus limiting the number of participants on this excursion.

Piraña Tour is a privately operated, community-supported enterprise, established after the failure of a communally–run program. César Piaguaje and Gilberto Piguaje (César`s brother-in-law) are certified by CETUR and INEFAN for guiding in the Cuyabeno Wildlife Reserve. The two are knowledgeable in both the cultural and scientific descriptions of their surroundings. Piraña Tour employs community members for various tasks and rents equipment (boats with motors) from them as well. The community of Siecoya and the Siecoya organization, OISE, receive portions of an entrance fee when groups are brought to the community. So far, the program has run smoothly and has been quite successful, attracting tourists from Europe and North America.

César meets guests in Lago Agrio and from there, arranges for a *ranchera* to take visitors to Puerto Chiritza or Poza Honda, from where they travel two to three hours downriver. Groups can range in size from four to 15 people, but six to eight people assure the best use of resources available. Young children are discouraged.

César Piaguaje´s warm sense of humor, wealth of knowledge, and open-mindedness make this tour program exceptional. He is willing to go to great lengths to make guests feel welcome and at ease. His desire for cultural exchange will have you deep in conversation about your home and his until late every night!

Price: $40 to $50/person/day (depending on group size, four day program), $55 to $65/person/day (depending on group size: five or more, eight day program). Add another $10/person/day on average if you require a bilingual naturalist guide to accompany your group (available via Tropic).

Contact: Piraña Tour, Manuel Silva, Casa de la Cultura, Colombia y 18 de Noviembre, Lago Agrio, Sucumbíos, tel: (06) 830 624, telefax: (06) 830 115, or Tropic Ecological Adventures, Av. Republica 307 y Almagro, Edif. Taurus, Dpto. 1-A, Quito, tel: (593 2) 225 907, 234 594, fax: (593 2) 560 756, e-mail: tropic@uio.satnet.net, www.tropiceco.com

PLAYAS DE CUYABENO

The Quichua community of Playas de Cuyabeno is strategically located at the confluence of the Ríos Cuyabeno and Aguarico in the core of the Cuyabeno Wildlife Reserve. A series of new *cabañas* on the lower Cuyabeno, within one hour of the community, give access to quiet blackwater lagoons, wilderness hikes and abundant wildlife. So far, this relatively new CBE project is only accessible to those making their own arrangements or asking a tour company.

The village of Playas is located on the Aguarico, surrounded by a strip of farmland and adjacent to small posts of INEFAN and the military, which control river traffic in the Reserve. The Flotel, a mobile floating hotel of Transturi, normally anchors within sight of the village.

Tourists have been visiting the area with tour agencies since the late 1970s, but community involvement in tourism only began with the arrival of the Flotel in 1991. Until two years ago, community members worked mostly as Flotel laborers receiving few benefits. In 1996, residents launched their own CBE program. Through community work days (*minga*) they built a network of four clean, solid *cabañas* and several dugout paddle canoes. The community recently added an eleven-story canopy observation tower built around a tall *ceibo* tree, the only communally owned structure of its type in the Reserve. The *cabañas* have separate dining/cooking and sleeping areas and are linked by boardwalks to latrines. One *cabaña* has flush toilets. Small docks with staircases provide access to the river. The three *cabañas* located on the Río Cuyabeno can be reached by motorized or dugout paddle canoe year round. Access to the fourth *cabaña* on the Río

Balatayacu may require a two-hour hike from the Río Cuyabeno, depending on water levels. It is wise to tow a dugout paddle canoe up the Cuyabeno in order to lazily float back down.

Since the infrastructure was established, the community has been able to negotiate a formal contract with Transturi. They now lodge travel agency groups and work as native guides on a weekly basis. Two members of the community completed a two–month guiding course, and shared their knowledge with the rest of the community. Thus, the entire adult population is now able to guide tours on a rotational basis, and many have begun English lessons. The *cabañas* are permanently staffed by families who rotate on a bi-monthly basis in order to minimize disruption of their daily routines. Their presence in the *cabañas* adds a cultural element to the tourism experience. Benefits are distributed equally within the community.

Millay Sacha ("Brave Jungle" in Quichua) is an appropriate name for this new ecotourism program. Despite its success, the community hopes for more control over tourism activities, yet still faces many barriers. Of primary concern is the lack of reliable communication with the tourism market. A radio in the community or regular staffing at the INEFAN station would help alleviate this problem. At the time of our visit, the community did not own basic equipment such as mattresses, mosquito nets or a communal motor canoe to transport tourists.

The ideal length of stay in Playas is three to five days. This time frame permits leisurely exploration of the lower reaches of the Río Cuyabeno by dugout paddle canoe or along trails. The community can receive groups of 4 to 20, larger groups being preferred. The ecotourism complex can sleep up to 80. As the community's program only runs activities for groups of 4 to 20 people, the surplus space is used by incoming tour agencies.

Playas de Cuyabeno received approximately 1 000 visitors in 1997-98.

Karen Chávez, the community's ecotourism coordinator, was enthusiastic about receiving independent tourists. A very informal program can be tailored to fit their needs. This type of tourist will no doubt play an important role in helping the community shift towards greater self management. Arriving well equipped is the key to successfully visiting this area on one's own (see Chapter XI; "Tips for Travelers"). The additional organizational hassles required may ultimately allow greater flexibility in programming than one would find through an agency.

Normal access is from Lago Agrio, by *ranchera* to either Chiritza (east of Lago Agrio) or Poza Honda (east of Shushufindi). From there, one may hire a motorized canoe for the three to four–hour ride to Playas. It is best to inquire in advance about transportation schedules and motorized canoe operators in Lago Agrio. Saturday is market day in Poza Honda and river traffic is at its highest, increasing the chances for arranging transportation. To ensure your return transportation from the community, it is probably best to negotiate with the motor canoe driver you arrive with.

The community may be contacted several ways. The most direct would be to contact the INEFAN office in Lago Agrio to relay a message to the Playas INEFAN post which, when staffed, is equipped with a radio. You can also send a message through Transturi which ferries passengers twice weekly to the Flotel. But don't rely on it! Several other tour operators use the community's facilities: Selvanieve, Harpiatour, Soltour and Native Life. All of these may be contacted in Quito.

Price: $65/person/day (group of five for four days) including transport from Lago Agrio.

Contact: Karen Chávez, Playas de Cuyabeno, c/o INEFAN, Calle 10 de Agosto entre Manabi y Colombia, Lago Agrio, Sucumbíos
Map: Q111-A3 CUYABENO

ZÁBALO

The longest-standing and most organized CBE program in the Río Aguarico region is run by the Cofan of Zábalo who occupy a remote part of the Cuyabeno Wildlife Reserve (Map 3). Randy Borman, the son of American missionaries who married a Cofan, is the community chief. He has developed an excellent tourism program with high-class accommodations. This conservation-minded community is mainly for those who are willing to pay for a quality experience in one of the Ecuadorian Amazon's most "wild" places.

Since 1978, when Borman and a small group of Cofan left the community of Dureno in search of wilderness far away from the impacts of the oil industry and encroaching settlement, they have been experimenting with various forms of managing their tourism operation. The complex current arrangements include community-owned and managed *cabañas*, Randy's community enterprise, a group operation, a private *cabaña* of a community member on the Río Zabalo, and a dysfunctional joint venture with Metropolitan touring. The community also offers a museum and an open handicraft market. Tourists interested in the problems and prospects of CBE can pump Randy´s extraordinary insight.

The community, bordered on one side by the Río Aguarico and on the other by pristine rainforest, is located three to five hours downriver from Chiritza, and one hour beyond the community of Playas de Cuyabeno. Between 1991 and 1993, it experienced major conflict with intruding oil companies. In October 1993 nearly all the men and women from the village, together with Andy Drumm of Acción Amazonía, hiked for two days through flooded forest to the site of an illegal oil rig on the edge of the Cofan territory. The drilling was halted by direct action, an unprecedented event in Ecuador. This era of Cofan history has been documented by Tidwell (1995). Since this time, the Cofan of Zábalo have done their best to conserve their environment, while maintaining controlled subsistence hunting.

If you are looking for comfort, Zábalo is the place to be! The communally-owned tourism infrastructure is located just outside the settlement along a soccer field in a tranquil forest clearing. The four *cabañas* are new, in excellent condition and very cozy. Each sleeping *cabaña* has two rooms each containing two single beds with thick mattresses and mosquito nets. Located behind these are the restrooms, with one shower, two flush toilets and a sink. A new dining *cabaña* with a kitchen and an eating area are under construction. It is to be hoped that the somewhat unimaginative food improves accordingly.

Three unique and excellent tourist programs are offered at Zábalo. "The Ecosystems" is a six-day program involving a canoe ride down the Río Zábalo and hiking through a beautiful rainforest, including a free day to pursue activities of personal interest. There is much scope for leisure including paddling around in a small dugout canoe, fishing, hiking, exploring the community, or just kicking back and relaxing. If you are lucky, a trip highlight will be spotting manatees and pink freshwater dolphins at the river mouths.

The second program, "The Black Lagoon", also lasts six days. Tourists travel one and a half hours upstream by motorized canoe to Shashamboe, a rustic camp on the Río Zábalo. An open, thatched roof sleeping *cabaña*, a dining *cabaña* with an open cooking fire, and a simple latrine serve as accommodations. The camp is equipped with thermarest mattresses and cooking facilities, although you must bring your own mosquito net. This is an excellent spot to seek out some of the many species of monkeys, including the Brown Woolly, Howler, Squirrel, Titi, Capuchin and Black mantled Tamarin. Watch out for the White-lipped peccaries!

Zábalo's third organized program, "Dancing Waters", includes five days of activities. Tourists travel to Baileplaya, a *cabaña* located on the Río Aguarico, upriver from the community. This program mixes jungle hiking with excursions by canoe, providing the opportunity to see monkeys, caimans, birds and butterflies and perhaps do a little piranha fishing.

Various other attractions are optional, such as the native art museum and handicraft market located across the Río Aguarico approximately five minutes upriver from the community. In addition, a turtle nursery project exists in Zábalo. It was implemented seven years ago with the help of Fundación Natura but is now managed independently, living proof of the community's commitment to fauna protection. Once a year young turtles are released to survive on their own in the wild.

For the dedicated and ambitious hiker, two optional, guided multiple-day treks through the forest towards the north are also possible. Three deteriorated, simple *cabañas* are located along this trail for overnight use. A feature attraction of this hike is a (secure) treetop rope and pulley system where guests are individually hoisted up, providing a remarkable view of the forest canopy and surrounding landscape. Ten to 15 minutes suffices for most tourists as they skeptically consider the minute apparatus on which their life depends. This region comprises 45 km of harsh trails - and is most suitable for those who are in good physical condition.

All programs include transportation, accommodation, food and guides. The above programs vary in content, so talk to Randy to make sure you choose the one best suited to your interests - he is extremely flexible and quite ready to accommodate tourist requests. Keep in mind that activities may vary with the seasons. The wet season is an ideal visiting period since more areas are reachable by boat and temperatures are relatively cool. The dry season is characterized by abundant insects near the river; however, a greater number of hiking trails are accessible. There is no set required group size, but eight people is ideal. If you go alone, expect to pay extra.

Zábalo deals with the following operators: Wilderness Travel, Harpia Tours, Tropic Ecological Adventures and Transturi. Community members are highly involved in their ecotourism project. With the exception of Randy and Rafael (who speaks reasonable English), the guides only speak Spanish and Cofan, but can utter some animal names in English.

If you do not wish to go with a tour, it is possible to access the community of Zábalo on your own. Take a *ranchera* from Lago Agrio to Puerta Chiritza (east of Lago Agrio) or Poza Honda (east of Shushufindi), then hire a canoe to take you the four hours down the Río Aguarico. Bring plenty of cash as gas does not come cheap!

Price: $60 to $120/person/day (depending on group size and program).
Contact: Randy Borman, fax: (593 2) 437 844,
e-mail: randyborman@earthlink.net,
http://www.genetic-id-services.com/cofan
Tropic Ecological Adventures, tel. (593 2) 234 594, 225 907,
fax (593 2) 560 756, e-mail: tropic@uio.satnet.net,
http://www.tropiceco.com

OYACACHI

If hot springs, mountains, waterfalls and ruins appeal to you, this highland Quichua community is definitively worth a visit. Located in the Cayambe-Coca Ecological Reserve, east of Quito in the transition from the *páramo* to the cloud forest, Oyacachi offers impressive scenery and a network of trails for adventurous, physically fit travelers. Since the village is not located in the tropical rainforest, it offers an alternative view of indigenous culture and ecotourism attractions, from those presented in this book.

Oyacachi can be reached via a side road that branches south from the Quito-Cayambe stretch of the Pan-American Highway. The community is divided into two small settlements, which are approximately one and a half kilometers apart, on the north side of the Oyacachi river. The main road reaches the first settlement; the other is only accessible by mule path. Two scenic hiking trails from Papallacta in the south and El Chaco in the southeast also lead to the community. Extended hiking trips can be arranged along these trails, ranging from two to seven days.

Several shorter trails extend throughout the region. One can hike four kilometers eastwards on the south shore of the Río Oyacachi to ancient ruins or take a shorter walk further north, up the main road to 11 different waterfalls. The photo opportunities are endless! A good hike to the southwest will lead you to numerous lagoons scattered throughout the *páramo*. Visitors have the opportunity to ride on horseback within these areas for $6 per day.

If you need a guide to take you hiking, look for David Parion who lives in the first village. If available, he can take you on single or multi-day hikes down the valley to El Chaco, but the traveler must bring all of his/her own camping and trekking gear. For those who prefer a more independent approach, a "do-it-yourself" program can be easily arranged.

There are no tourist facilities other than three changing and washing complexes near the hot springs and bathrooms through-out the village. A small kitchenette (infrequently used) is available near the springs, where one can also set up a tent. Only a limited variety of food can be purchased in the community; so it is best to come prepared.

A few years ago three thermal baths were built on the south side of the Río Oyacachi. They have been sadly neglected and at present only one is being maintained, and available for a modest daily fee of $0.20.

You will also experience truly authentic handicrafts, food and dress. Beautiful wood carvings of local animals (owls, bears and the Andean Condor) can be seen and purchased; don't leave without one of their specialties: giant wooden spoons! For gen-uine Oyacachi cuisine, look for Gonzalo Parion, the cheese maker, from whom you can buy a round of cheese for $1. While savoring this tasty treat, you may be struck by the traditional female costume of colorful skirts, bright ponchos, and wrapped ribbons in long, straight or braided hair.

As a community based project, Oyacachi is still in its early stages of development. Although tourists have passed through for many years and people from neighboring communities regularly visit the hot springs on weekends, specific programs have yet to be established. Community leaders, however, are very enthusias-tic and seem eager to start a program which will directly benefit the village.

Access to the community is a bit tricky. The quickest way is by bus from Quito to Cayambe (about two hours). From there, you will have to ask around about rides to Oyacachi. There is a bus, but it does not have a regular schedule, so don't count on finding it. Another option, although more expensive, would be to take a taxi. Fortunately, hitchhiking is feasible; so catching a ride, on a cheese truck perhaps, is a possibility. If you are heading back to Cayambe after your visit, you should consider walking, to fully appreciate the spectacular scenery of the mountains and the sprawling patchwork of agricultural land. The walk takes about six hours, but it's all downhill and the dirt road is easy to follow.

Price: Negotiated on site. $2 per day entrance fee.
Contact: Ecocienca, Isla San Cristóbal 1523 y Seymour, Casilla 17-12-257, Quito, telefax: (593 2) 451 338, 451 338

VIII
COMMUNITY BASED ECOTOURISM
IN THE MIDDLE AND LOWER NAPO REGION

The Middle and Lower Napo and southern tributaries region is a sparsely populated lowland area, shared by the Quichua and Huaorani and two protected areas: Limoncocha Biological Reserve, the second smallest, and Yasuní National Park, the largest nature reserve in Ecuador (Maps 2, 3). The western portion of the region is dominated by settlers, oil wells and pipelines, while the bulk remains in virgin forest occasionally broken by islands of subsistence farming and small-scale agriculture. It is a tragedy that Yasuní National Park, a UNESCO Biosphere Reserve, is being exploited by international oil companies such as ELF-Aquitaine, YPF and Perez Compac. It is doubtful that American and European car drivers are aware of the destruction being wreaked in the name of cheap oil. Most of the park is still pristine, but action will have to be taken soon if we are to save this jewel of biodiversity.

Most of the area is dominated by rivers: the Napo, the Tiputini, the Shiripuno, and the Yasuní in the heart of the Park which bears its name. Ridges and hills characterize the west while lowlands and swampy areas define much of the unexplored and biodiverse east.

The gateway city to this area is Coca, a dirty, rough, oil boom town which provides adequate services, though far more rudimentary than those of Tena, Lago Agrio or Puyo. This town offers very few acceptable hotels with the exception of "La Misión", a safe, clean and pleasant place to stay, frequented by American soldiers, oil workers and environmentalists. Be sure to change your money before arrival as banking services are poor and the exchange rates are rarely in the tourist's favor.

Travel to CBE locations and the area's parks is from Coca, mainly by river. The Río Napo carries tourists to the most popular locales, while the southern tributaries lend access to Yasuní National Park and the Huaorani communities. Limoncocha Biological Reserve, accessible via the Río Napo, or by road via Shushufindi, was created in 1985 to protect the 28 000 hectares of rainforest surrounding the Limoncocha Lagoon. In the 1980s seismic work and drilling by Oxy affected the wildlife. The construction of an oil production facility and oil wells just 100 meters away from the lagoon and the construction of a road network has permanently reduced wildlife abundance, though caiman and Hoatzin can still be found here.

With a total area of 982 300 hectares, Yasuní National Park extends southward into Pastaza province (Maps 2, 3, 4, 5) and embodies wetlands, marshes, swamps, lakes, river systems and rainforest. Established in 1979, it is home to jaguars, pumas, giant armadillos, parrots, 10 species of monkeys as well as caimans and numerous endemic species which are part of its world class biodiversity. For this reason, Yasuní was declared an international biosphere reserve by the UNESCO (United Nations Educational, Social and Cultural Organization).

The two parks are fully buffered by an unbroken chain of Quichua territories along the Río Napo, and the extensive Huaorani reserve west of Yasuní National Park. This strategic indigenous control of vast, virtually untouched land bodes well for future CBE development. For the moment, however, the region has only a small number of CBE projects, most being of very recent origin or in the process of implementation. When all facilities are completed as planned, an interesting range of offerings

will be available in the wildest and least explored region of
Ecuador!

Yuca plant
(K. Bemben)

AMAZANGA

Amazanga is working to offer a range of tours within the area of influence of FCUNAE, the Quichua federation of the Middle and Lower Napo. Owned by members of the Quichua community Armenia, Amazanga is a private enterprise that operates in conjunction with FCUNAE, serving as its tourism operator. This arrangement is much like the one Papangu Tours has with ATACAPI in Pastaza province. The group leads well organized and economical tours through the western and interior portion of Yasuní National Park and potentially into the Sumaco-Galeras National Park. Although programs are still being planned in some cases, the strong leadership of Amazanga's president, César Andy, shows potential for further tourism development in the remote areas of Napo province.

All tours begin in Coca where Amazanga is based. Several tours head down the Río Napo to Quichua communities and lagoons, others head south of the city along the Vía Auca and descend the Río Tiputini system into Yasuní National Park. Yet others head west to the Río Payamino. An exciting wilderness program to the northern tip of the Sumaco-Galeras National Park is planned for the future.

Although Amazanga owns mosquito nets, rubber boots, sleeping pads, lifejackets, cooking materials, one or two large rafts and dugout paddle canoes, participants may wish to bring their personal equipment. Amazanga is making plans for the construction of new *cabañas* along the lagoons, rivers and sections of forest that it visits; but in the meantime, tourists are mainly housed in the homes of Quichua community members.

In January 1998, César Andy struck an agreement with FCUNAE to operate tourism programs according to the organization's constitution. Communities that receive tourists through Amazanga benefit by being paid an entrance fee when a tour passes through. FCUNAE receives a portion of all profits and the rest goes to the entrepreneurs. At present, there are two licensed guides who speak Quichua and Spanish with two more to be added soon. Coupled with the biology and ecotourism program of the technical secondary school of the Quichua community of Armenia (where Amazanga originated), this tourism agency has a qualified human resource base for future expansion.

Trips vary anywhere from three to nine days in length, and can be combined for even longer stays. Programs begin with a day of travel to the site (either by *ranchera*, on foot or by river), followed by a reception performed by the host community. The core of any program enables tourists to visit a specific natural attraction every day, with small demonstrations by the guides while walking or paddling. Piranha fishing, caiman spotting and bird watching are all possible, depending on the specialization of the guide and the tour selected. The second last day is reserved for small excursions, community demonstrations and intercultural exchange. Free time can be spent swimming, reading or resting.

These tours are ideal for travelers already in Coca. While in the city, head to the waterfront, upriver from the bridge across the Napo. There you will find Amazanga's offices near the port captaincy (*capitanía del puerto*); there are a few offices here, so check signs carefully. If the offices are locked, check in the small indigenous restaurant next door for a representative (the *chicha* is fantastic!). Amazanga prefers reservations; however, they can accommodate unannounced arrivals. Tourist groups normally range from five to 12 people. Keep in mind that larger groups will bring prices down, while programs requiring more physical mobility are more easily executed with fewer participants.

Amazanga is new to the industry, experiencing the same "growing pains" as the other groups operating on the Middle and Lower Napo. Nonetheless, for the backpacking ecotourist on a budget, Amazanga is an enthusiastic enterprise with strong links to the remote communities it serves, so poking your nose around in Coca to see how they are coming along might yield some pleasant surprises!

Price: Approx. $35 to $40 person/day (at present, a price structure is not fixed).
Contact: César Andy, Amazanga, Coca, Provincia de Orellana, Tel: (06) 880 833, 880 663, 880 046, 880 495

AÑANGU

Birders will want to flock to Añangu at the thought of its extraordinary birdlife! This Quichua community controls an enchanting lagoon in the northwestern tip of Yasuní National Park, three hours downriver from Coca (Map 3), where over 400 bird species have been identified. A prominent community member, Giovani Calapuacha, has worked extensively with larger tourism operations such as La Selva Lodge, and is renowned as one of Ecuador's top birders. Taking his experience from upscale operators nearby, combined with his superior bird watching skills, Giovani now hopes to build the birder's dream come true.

The community of Añangu is on the south shore of the Río Napo between Sacha and La Selva Lodges. While the community center and dispersed houses are aligned on the riverbank, the tourism *cabaña* is situated on Añangucocha, one of the largest lagoons in Napo province. To get there one must hike for one hour from the drop-off point on the Río Napo, followed by 20 minutes of paddling (longer if you get stuck when the water levels are low!) across the lagoon to the *cabaña*. The current tourism infrastructure consists of a single thatched, open-sided *cabaña* sheltering a ground-level cooking section and two raised sleeping platforms with a maximum capacity of eight people. There are no washroom facilities.

Giovani envisions complete replacement of the tourism infrastructure so as to be able to host a total of 20 people. Assuming proper financing, the first part of the project will be to build a cooking/dining facility, a bar, and five double *cabañas* with private bathrooms and showers at the lagoon. Once completed, a similar complex is planned along the Río Napo, east of the community, near a riverside cliff where a host of birds congregate at a salt lick (*saladero*). An observation tower is to be built in this location as well. The comfort and quality of the new buildings are to be similar to the neighboring upscale La Selva and Sacha Lodges. This project is scheduled to begin during the summer of 1998, and to be completed within one year. To what extent the dream will turn into reality remains to be seen.

The lagoon of Añangucocha, around which the present program is based, is idyllic. Its waters and bordering wetlands are home to caimans, piranhas, turtles and the legendary *"paiche"* (a 200 pound fish). In the surrounding tropical rainforest roam animals such as pumas, peccaries, and monkeys. Biologists and weekend birders will find Giovani's expertise and representations to provide an exciting learning experience. Hoatzins, egrets, and toucans are some of the common species to be spotted. As mentioned earlier, 400 species have been identified in this area alone. Given Yasuní National Park's reputation, you may spot number 401! Other activities include casual jungle walks and medicinal plant observation and explanation. Swimming and paddling in the lagoon are also possible during leisure time.

At present, programs are flexible and can be designed to meet the tourist's desires. In the future, a structured eight-day program is to be implemented including both existing and additional activities. Cultural programming such as a mock wedding ceremony, a blowgun demonstration and a visit to the community of Sani Isla will be added to keep the operation competitive with the more established tourist sites. At present tourists must bring their own food and equipment; however, in the future all will be provided.

At present a fee of $20 per night per group is paid into the community fund for the use of the community's *cabaña* and territory. Plans state that the newly formed association of 10 members, which is coordinating the remodeling of the tourism infrastructure and programs, will pay a fixed monthly rent to the Añangu community for the use of its communal land. These profits will most likely benefit local education, health and development programs. The members will receive priority for employment and training by Giovani. Note that the community has already approved the project and is eager to participate.

Access to Añangu is, at present, somewhat problematic. Potential visitors can first attempt to contact the community by radio at frequency #246 from the INEFAN office in either Coca or Limoncocha to alert them of their arrival. After this, the most certain way to travel to the community, but also the most expensive, is by river from Coca. You can try your luck bartering for a canoe, but may end up paying $100 one-way. Cheaper and faster, but less predictable access is from the Pompeya market (Map 3) which is located on the Río Napo at the end of the Shushufindi - Limoncocha road (about four hours by bus from Coca, with waiting). Canoes leave before 11 am on Sunday, when people return downriver after attending the market in the early morning. Finally, there is a very cheap, primitive weekly passenger boat which travels from Coca to Nueva Rocafuerte (passing by Añangu) which is easier on the budget. Be sure to check with the port authority regarding the passenger boat schedule. Note that any travelers leaving by boat from Coca require a permit from INEFAN and the port authority.

Añangu is a wonderful place to experience the sounds of the jungle and lagoon inhabited by a diversity of wildlife; waking to the sound of Howler monkeys is an exciting but slightly alarming experience! A camera and binoculars are essential to fully enjoy the beautiful surroundings and the breathtaking sunrises and sunsets over the lagoon. Note that community members are flexible and will accommodate spontaneous arrivals. Plan on a minimum three-day stay.

Price: Currently $20/night/group (irrespective of size), $10/guide/day, plus river transportation which varies. Future program prices have not been established, but will include transportation from Coca.

White cocoa
(K. Bemben)

QUEHUEIRE'ONO

Readers of Joe Kane's book <u>Savages</u> will recognize Quehueire'ono as the home of Moi Enomenga and the Huaos with whom the author traveled for over two years. Today, Quehueire'ono is the first Huaorani community to establish a self-reliant ecotourism program in partnership with Tropic Ecological Adventures and led by Moi Enomenga himself. The community is situated on both banks of the Río Shiripuno at the northwestern edge of the Huaorani territory. The community has adopted an ecotourism strategy that discourages the proliferation of oil exploration and encroaching colonists while educating visitors about the abundance of the jungle and the ways of the only indigenous group to never have been conquered.

Trips begin with a drive through the Avenue of the Volcanoes south of Quito, then over the eastern cordillera and down the spectacular Pastaza river valley into the Amazon to the frontier town of Shell. Here, while you lunch at a local restaurant, Tropic's bilingual naturalist guide sorts out the necessary ONHAE and military permits and loads up the five-seater aircraft for a breathtaking 45-minute flight over the seemingly endless rainforest canopy until the tiny clearing that is Quehueire'ono appears. On arrival the entire community appears from their homes to greet the visitors and Community Ecotourism Coordinator and local guide Moi introduces himself.

The community itself consists of houses spread along the riverbanks and a village centered around the airstrip and communal area where Huaorani children play. The tourism complex is 45 minutes away by foot, or one hour by manually poled canoe from the community. The accommodations are built in the local

Huaorani style with thatched roofs that extend to the ground. A raised sleeping platform has been included for added comfort. There is a sleeping hut for eight people, with cooking and dining huts and two latrines nearby. Washing is done in the river, so don't forget your biodegradable soap!

Tourists can choose between visits of four to seven days with Tropic Ecological Adventures in Quito. The ecotourism program bases its jungle activities near the Río Shiripuno where a wide variety of fauna and flora may be observed. Itineraries may be modified to suit the specific interests of the tourists, given proper notice. On the seven-day program, tourists normally travel by road to Shell near Puyo (Map 2) and fly to the Shiripuno by single engine aircraft. They spend the next two days visiting the communities of Quehueire'ono and Wentaro. A four-hour jungle walk upstream between the two will introduce tourists to the Huaorani territory. A rich cultural program exposes visitors to various facets of Huao life: blowgun demonstrations, fire making, hammock weaving, food preparation and home construction. During the evenings, tourists can converse with their Huaorani guide on Huaorani culture and spiritual beliefs.

On the fourth day, tourists begin their two-night adventure by poling down the Shiripuno in a *quilla*. Activities during this portion of the trip include moderate jungle walks, fishing, and visits to a lagoon and an oxbow lake, all of which take place at various stops on the way down. Regardless of the length of their stay in Huaorani territory, tourists will get a glimpse of various birds and animals as well as explanations of uses of medicinal plants and trees. A Huaorani guide will provide detailed explanations of all of these as they relate to Huaorani daily life. In the evenings, visitors are free to relax, but there are options to take short night walks. Poling downriver is definitely the way to appreciate the natural sounds and rythms of the forest – no noisy outboard motors! The sheltered river is pretty, but notorious for being plugged by large trees due to riverbank erosion; this makes navigation a little more challenging here than on other rivers. Eventually the forest opens up as the Via Auca and the oil pipeline is reached. Tropic's transport is waiting to take you to Coca, with stops to fully comprehend the impact of this highway, of the oil pipeline running alongside it, and of unchecked colonization on the Huaorani people. Tourists will spend the final night in the comfortable "La Misión" hotel, and return to Quito the next day on a scheduled flight.

Quehueire'ono's ecotourism program is an exclusive joint venture operation with Tropic Ecological Adventures. This company is committed to principles of sustainability, ensuring that the community and the ONHAE (Organization of the Huaorani Nationality of the Ecuadorian Amazon), receive proper economic benefits, unlike other less scrupulous tour operators currently working in Huaorani territory. Ultimately, the Quehueire'ono ecotourism program will become an independent CBE organization as the Huaorani acquire more experience in the industry. The community manages all river transportation, and assists with meal preparation. Tropic provides a head/training cook.

The combination of a local Huaorani guide who can share the perspective of the rainforest from the inside with a bilingual naturalist guide who provides ecological depth and context is a good one. The community would ideally like to receive one group of three to eight tourists per month. Spontaneous arrivals are not feasible, as strict visitation limits are in place, and the need for adequate preparation for visitors in the community.

It is important to note that the Huaorani are the indigenous group that has been the least exposed to tourists. Visitors must follow the example of their guide and ask prior to doing anything outside of the programmed activities, in order to avoid any confusion and misunderstandings that could lead to uncomfortable situations. Also, keep in mind that although a large part of the community's nutrition is based on hunting and forest products, food and drinking water for visitors is brought from Quito to reduce pressure on the local environment.

When visiting Quehueire'ono, tourists must remember that they are now on "Huaorani Time". This community offers a unique experience for those who seek and can embrace the Huaorani way. So when you ask your Huaorani guide what time it is, be flexible, open-minded and just smile if he replies "it's 2:00 in Tokyo…"

Price: From $75 to $150/person/day according to group size and program.
Contact: Tropic Ecological Adventures, Av. República 307 y Almagro, Edif. Taurus, Dpto. 1-A, Quito, tel.: (593 2) 225 907, 234 594, fax: (593 2) 560 756, e-mail: tropic@uio.satnet.net, www.tropiceco.com

IX
COMMUNITY BASED ECOTOURISM
IN THE UPPER NAPO REGION

The Upper Napo is the core area of the Quijos Quichua. It comprises the western part of Napo province and corresponds to the headwaters of the Río Napo. The region is framed by the steeply descending eastern slopes of the Andes to the west, and by the Sumaco-Galeras National Park to the north and the east (Map 4). The inhabited portion corresponds to the Andean piedmont, where a checkerboard of settler and Quichua territory (depicted in simplified fashion in Map 4) has emerged. The indigenous population of the Upper Napo is exclusively Quichua, and thus all CBE projects listed below are in Quichua communities.

Tena, the capital of Napo province, is the region's administrative and service center. It offers a greater range of services and a more staid and pleasant atmosphere than the oil centers of Lago Agrio and Coca. It is the hub of an extensive local road network, which is grafted onto the north-south road leading from Baeza to Puyo. Many of the indigenous settlements and several CBE projects are accessible by road. Branch roads reach the ports of Misahuallí and Ahuano on the Río Napo, connecting to downriver navigation.

The settled parts of the region have a pleasant, rolling landscape where patches of forest are intermixed with pasture and cropland. Throughout the area forested mountain ranges form the backdrop. Rushing rivers, pebble and/or sand beaches, rapids and waterfalls, permit a variety of water-related activities such as climbing up enchanted valleys, swimming, tubing and rafting.

To the north and east, the national park Sumaco-Galeras has considerable potential for trekking. The centerpiece is the perfect cone of the Sumaco Volcano, which in 1997 was visited by only 30 to 40 tourists but is soon to be made more accessible through a trail and a series of *cabañas*.

The park embraces largely unexplored wilderness which has escaped the threat of colonization and oil development. The wildlife is not frightened when approached, which indicates that hunting is not a common practice. The area is mostly untouched and lacks trails; it is therefore very difficult to access without the assistance of a trained guide. To the west, the Cordillera Huacamayos, a front range of the Andes, is equally inviting.

Both of these areas are now part of sustainable development projects based on a buffer zone concept, which integrates adjacent Quichua communities. In either case indigenous communities and CBE projects are located in the buffer zones outside the areas which are to be protected.

The region is an excellent base for CBE excursions due to the multitude of options within a few hours and in some cases, minutes from Tena. Despite encroaching colonization and oil expansion, nearby communities have preserved their territory and cultures remakably well, safeguarding their authenticity. Most CBE enterprises are located along the Río Napo or near a local dirt road. Thus they are easily accessible either by bus, taxi or canoe. Most CBE enterprises work in conjunction with RICANCIE in Tena.

RICANCIE

In the Upper Napo region, CBE projects are perhaps most accessible through the nine communities that make up the RICANCIE network (Network of Indigenous Communities of the Upper Napo for Intercultural Exchange and Ecotourism). Operating out of Tena, RICANCIE has officially been providing quality indigenous-run ecotourism experiences since 1993, although Capirona (Map 4), the network's flagship program, has been in operation since 1990 (Colvin 1994, Wesche 1993, 1995, Izko 1995).

Capirona's initial involvement with ecotourism was a reluctant one, but was partially seen as a solution to a multitude of impacts, such as invasion of its territories by petroleum and logging companies, with the inevitable colonization that followed and the visits of unauthorized tourist groups from which they received no profits. It also provided a way for the community to diversify its economy when maize prices fell in the late 1980s. With start-up money provided by FOIN (Federation of Indigenous Organizations of Napo) and the nearby Jatun Sacha Foundation, Capirona was soon equipped to receive tourists. The initial success of its program inspired other communities faced with similar challenges, and in 1993, FOIN created RICANCIE to coordinate these communities' efforts. Since then RICANCIE has been able to obtain legal recognition of its operations which permits its member communities to gain a foothold into the tourism industry and financially profit from it. RICANCIE has provided guiding courses and continues to do so for the management of newly developed CBE projects.

The nine communities presently involved in the network offer a wide range of activities and program lengths to suit all from the most timid time/money conscious travelers to hardcore cavers looking to drop into new pits and map new passages. Cultural presentations exposing the local Quichua way of life are offered in every community but are the specialty of some, such as Cuya Loma (see "Features of CBE Projects" in Appendix 1). Lodging in comfortable, traditional thatched roof *cabañas* with beds, sheets and mosquito nets is a standard for all programs. Rubber boots are provided in most sizes, but it might be safer to bring your own. Satisfying meals made with both local and non-local ingredients are included in the prices, and vegetarians can be catered to if your guide is advised ahead of time. It is possible to link visits between most of the network's communitites. Such combinations as well as all bookings and logistics are presently arranged through RICANCIE's office in Tena.

Prices for all nine programs are fixed. For visitors planning a stay of more than two days, a single package price of $60/day/person is offered. This fee includes all transportation costs from Tena, food, accomodations, guides and cultural presentations and is the most hassle-free way to pay. An itemized fee structure is also available for students and budget-conscious travelers. This allows you to select cheaper options such as public transportation, or to altogether skip activities such as cultural presentations. Although more affordable, this option contributes little to the local indigenous economy or to RICANCIE's future existence, which is unfortunately never secure.

Price: $60/ person/ day package (or selected services at lower price)

Contact: RICANCIE , Av. 15 de Noviembre 772, Casilla Postal 243, Tena, Napo, telefax: (06) 887-072

Gracious host, indigenas of Ecuador's Oriente *(G. Renart)*

Thankful guest from Canada, the University of Ottawa team *(J. McArthur)*

King of the jungle - the ceibo tree *(J. McArthur)*

Amazonian playground
Ricardo Ushigua climbs
a matapalo tree
(N. Ayotte)

Cesario Piaguaje
- Siecoya shaman
(A. Drumm)

Quichua children in Capirona
(R. Zalatan)

Signs of acculturation typical of the
Upper Napo Quichua (Settler style
home and coffee drying for sale)
(S. St-Michel)

A Siona medicinal healing ritual
in Orahuëyá keeps traditional culture
alive with the new generation
(R. Zalatan)

Relaxing Quichua style in Playas de Cuyabeno *(I. Gariépy)*

Huaorani children along
the Río Shiripuno
(J. McArthur)

Signs of "modernization" in a Huaorani home *(J. McArthur)*

Huaorani leader Moi Enomenga, making a crown for a cultural presentation in Quehueire'ono
(M. Cyr)

Siesta time in the jungle for this little critter
(N. Ayotte)

Community members of Valle
Hermoso (Pavacachi)
(S. Wesche)

The detailed beauty of nature
(N. Ayotte)

Lisandro Piaguaje, a Biaña guide, tries out a tourist's taste for native dress
(J. McArthur)

A sunny afternoon of tubing on the Rio Tena near AACLLAC
(N. Ayotte)

Fishing for pirahna on the Rio Conambo
…but only the catfish were biting!!
(N. Ayotte)

Río Aguarico
(N. Ayotte)

The Chávez family
on the Río Cuyabeno
(I. Gariepy)

Cofan boy on the black waters
of the Rio Zábalo
(N. Ayotte)

Tourist in Huaorani territory on the
white waters of the Río Shiripuno
(A. Drumm)

Ruben Vargas (holding chicha bowl), President of the Achuar Asociación AMUNTI with his family in the community of Kapawi (S. Wesche)

Qhichua children crossing a stream in the community of Valle Hermoso [Pavacachi] (R. Zalatan)

Monkeys are part of the family...
(Left: J. Godin)   (Right: N. Ayotte)

Quichua potters shop in Santa Rita *(C. Jeanneret)*

Dinner by the fireside
San José de Puma Pungo
(D. Trépanier)

Scarlet Macaw in Pavacachi
(M. Cyr)

Some of Kapawi's ecolodge guest cabañas built in Achuar style,
hammocks and all (S. Wesche)

Sunset over
cultivated landscape
(J. McArthur)

Sunset from the Machacuyacu
Reserve
(D. Trépanier)

A Siona boy in Biaña with Pedro, his pet monkey
(J McArthur)

Záparo woman in Llanchamacocha mashing yuca for chicha. Many indigenous communities also puree the yuca by chewing it and spitting it back into the mixture
(N. Ayotte)

Siona cultural presentation in Biaña
(J. McArthur)

The seed of the achiote are used
as body paint in many communities
(J. McArthur)

Jungle romance - the beauty
of Salazar Aitaca's Copa Falls.
Spot the guide!
(I. Gariépy)

Oxbow lagoon near
Llanchamacocha - Spot the
caiman!!
(N. Ayotte)

Natural elegance - the color of life *(R. Zalatan)*

A tasty dinner of grubs (*gusanos*) and veggies in Unión Venecia
(N. Ayotte)

Capirona cuisine
(R. Zalatan)

The destruction in obvious... *(A. Drumm)*

The message is clear *(J. McArthur)*

Cabañas in the Cofan
community of Zábalo
(A. Drumm)

Cofan handicraft in Zábalo
(A.Drumm)

Bridge over Jatunyacu, Sapollo

(A. Drumm)

CUYA LOMA (RICANCIE)

Among the communities of the RICANCIE network, Cuya Loma is the most accessible, being located only 20 minutes east of Tena on the Misahuallí road. Visitors experience a unique program focused on the traditional Quichua culture which is authentically re-created during enthusiastic and realistic cultural presentations. Additionally, the community boasts an impressive archeological museum.

This CBE project is quite flexible, offering a variety of activities that can be experienced in an afternoon or during lengthier stays of up to three days. Cultural attractions include re-enactments of Quichua rituals, observation and description of medicinal plants and their use, and an educational tour of the museum. Displayed in the latter are traditional garments, kitchenware, a detailed small-scale model of a typical Quichua home, and hunting and fishing instruments. The community also has a wide selection of handicrafts for sale. Such cultural activities can be combined with moderate hikes through the surrounding tropical forest.

In addition to well-trained and knowledgeable guides, Cuya Loma offers very comfortable accommodations. Facilities were constructed in traditional thatched roof style, and consist of a sleeping *cabaña*, a kitchen/dining hall and a separate bathroom. The sleeping cabaña can accommodate up to seven people and bathroom facilities are equipped with running water. Future plans include the construction of new *cabañas* in a more secluded area near the Río Napo. The existing structure is to be designated as a healing center where tourists can attend shamanic demonstrations of medicinal plant healing. Also planned is the establishment of an ecological tourism circuit between the communities of Salazar Aitaca, Machacuyacu and Unión Venecia.

Apart from the museum, which is owned and managed by one family, Cuya Loma community members work on a rotational basis to fulfill all aspects of the project. Members directly involved in the program are paid a fixed salary whereas the remaining profits are invested directly in community development.

Arrangements can be made through RICANCIE, with a guide meeting you in Tena. Spontaneous arrivals are not a problem, since you may take a bus or taxi and ask the driver where to get off. A hidden staircase leads from the left side of the road up to the community. A visit to Cuya Loma is highly recommended as it offers an enlightened retrospective on the development of Quichua culture in the Napo region.

Map: CT OIV-A2 Puerto Misahuallí

UNIÓN VENECIA (RICANCIE)

Unión Venecia offers a comfortable, relaxing and easily accessible environment for a wide range of tourists, both young and old. Located east of Puerto Napo on the north bank of the Río Napo overlooking an island, this site is perfectly suited for relaxing on the beach while enjoying exceptionally well prepared typical food. Excellent guides and cooks offer quality service, providing an enjoyable stay for the tourist seeking an interactive experience with the Quichua culture.

The community is divided by the Río Napo, and most of the young people inhabit Venecia Izquierda (on the left shore of the Río Napo) while the elders have remained in Venecia Derecha (on the right shore). The slightly secluded tourism facilities, surrounded by small crops and secondary forest, are located one kilometer from the community center of Venecia Izquierda on the north bank of the river 400 m from the Pto. Misahuallí road.

Typically, programs run between two and five days. However, this is easily adjusted to meet the desires and capabilities of a range of tourists. Activities include a traditional Quichua music and dance program in which tourists are strongly encouraged to participate. Daytime activities include motor canoe rides on the Río Napo and tropical forest hikes through a network of trails varying in length and difficulty (typically lasting between one and five hours). A sandy beach lies next to the *cabañas*, providing a perfect site for bathing and for admiring sunsets over the distant Andean foothills. Meals in the community are a rare treat. These include an exquisite variety of local foods which are creatively prepared and served on beautiful, locally-made ceramic dishes, many of which are available for purchase in addition to other handicrafts.

The tourism complex consists of three well-maintained sleeping *cabañas* and a large dining room, with capacity for 14 guests. Unión Venecia requests groups with a minimum of four people. Groups larger than 14 can be accommodated in tents, if necessary. A separate *cabaña* contains a well-kept bathroom with sink and shower facilities. Rubber boots and life jackets are provided.

The community's involvement in ecotourism began in 1994 when it became part of the RICANCIE network. Part of the profits derived from the venture are re-invested into the program for overall maintenance or used for specific community needs. In the future, Unión Venecia plans to establish an "ecological circuit" with the communities of Salazar Aitaca, Machacuyacu, and Cuya Loma (Map 4). They also foresee building a boardroom for group meetings.

Unión Venecia is easily reachable by bus or taxi. The trailhead is located 30 minutes from Tena on the Misahuallí road. From there, a five-minute walk towards the river brings you to the *cabaña* complex.

Before you leave this waterfront paradise, don't forget to include your comments in the guest book. The community is eager to improve its services and will be delighted to consider your suggestions.

Map: CT OIV-A2 Puerto Misahuallí

MACHACUYACU (RICANCIE)

Machacuyacu (which translates to "River of the Snake" in Quichua), offers moderately difficult hikes across a diverse landscape, filled with challenging caves and spectacular views. The community is attractively located in an elevated region, approximately 15 km east of the city of Tena, just north of the Río Napo. There are several look-outs (*miradores*) throughout their territory which have impressive, panoramic views of the Río Napo valley, the eastern range of the Andes and the Cordillera Huacamayos.

A CBE program progressed in Machacuyacu as a result of active leadership and involvement with RICANCIE. Although much of the surrounding land has become agriculturally impacted, the area has much to offer in terms of natural and scenic attractions. The territory encompasses unexplored caves and a small reserve which fringes the Río Misahuallí.

The main tourism complex is located five minutes away from the community center and can be reached via a 45-minute walk from the Misahuallí road. Upon arrival, visitors may relax in the Río Machacuyacu, and later retreat to comfortable, clean *cabañas*. Another tourism *cabaña* is located on the higher grounds of the reserve. It offers spectacular views of the Sumaco Volcano, the Río Misahuallí valley and the Copayacu waterfalls and lagoon.

Machacuyacu has great potential for cave exploration, yet the tourist should be culturally sensitive to local myths involving caves. The local caves appear to be difficult to access and there is one in particular which has a large, deep mouth. Visitors may attend a variety of small presentations, such as blowgun demonstrations, spiritual ceremonies and hunting/fishing techniques.

Presently, there is one main tourism trail that climbs up to the reserve and down to the Río Misahuallí. It is a moderate four-hour climb up to the reserve and a two-hour trek down. For a more challenging experience, one can continue on a 30-minute abrupt descent to the Río Misahuallí from the *cabaña*. Two tents are also available for prolonged hiking excursions.

Several families that reside in the community center are actively involved in the tourism program and work on a rotational basis. They share half of the benefits while the remainder is spent on medical and educational needs for the entire community. There are two members of Machacuyacu who have received the RICANCIE training course and are qualified to lead interpretive hikes throughout the territory.

Visitors will be delighted with the accommodations which are available in the community. There are two spacious, well-maintained sleeping *cabañas* which accommodate six people as well as a tidy latrine. In the near future, the community plans to complete the construction of a dining hall, install a water tank and new washroom facilities with showers. Higher up in the reserve, there is a basic sleeping shelter with a latrine.

A major project underway is the completion of a footbridge over the Río Misahuallí (see "Salazar Aitaca"). As of now, tourists must swim if they wish to access the other side, as a canoe is not yet available to transport them across. This future bridge will provide permanent access between the communities of Salazar Aitaca, San José de Puma Pungo and Machacuyacu and facilitate an eventual joint, extended program to be organized throughout the region.

Maps: CT OIV-A2 Puerto Misahuallí; CT OIII-E4 Lushanta

RUNA HUASI (RICANCIE)

The community of 27 de Febrero operates the ecotourism project called Runa Huasi, which offers a picturesque locale from which one can leisurely take in the AmaZOOnico animal recovery station - a must for all animal lovers! The ornately decorated *cabañas* overlooking the lower Río Arajuno near Ahuano will complete your picture portfolio with fine landscapes and sunsets. Quickly accessed from Tena, Runa Huasi is the ideal escape, even if just for a night or two.

Programs are four to five days in length, the extra night consisting of a camping excursion in the jungle on the Río Nushiño. The main attraction of Runa Huasi is AmaZOOnico, the animal rehabilitation center. A short 10-minute walk from the Runa Huasi *cabañas*, the center, owned and managed by Swiss biologist Angelika Raimann and her Quichua husband Remigio Canelos, has been receiving mistreated local animals through the Ecuadorian government since 1993. The center houses the animals and frees them into the jungle when they are fit enough to be returned to the wild. Expect to see a wide variety of animals including monkeys, caimans, tapirs, jaguarundi, parrots, turtles, ocelots, macaws, owls and many more. Requests can be made for guided tours in English, French, Spanish, German or Quichua.

The remainder of the ecotourism program consists of hiking through 48 hectares of primary forest, where tourists will see a fossil lake, visit the bird look-out, and learn about local medicinal plants. In addition, visitors can savor traditional Quichua food at mealtimes. During their free time, tourists can swim, take in the scenery from patio hammocks, and in the near future, paddle small dugout canoes on the Río Arajuno.

The project's *cabañas* are elevated approximately 15 m above the river on the east side, facing the Isla Anaconda, where the members of the 27 de Febrero community live. To the east, behind the *cabañas* lies primary forest with the Ríos Rodriguez and Nushiño running parallel to the Arajuno. There are three *cabañas* sleeping 12 persons, all of which are comfortably equipped with sheets, pillows, mattresses and towels. Two have flush toilets, decorative showers and creatively designed balconies.

Twenty-two members of the 27 de Febrero participate actively in the project, rotating their work every two to three months and participating in a community work day together for larger projects. Enrique Tapuy is the licensed guide and speaks Quichua, Spanish and English. He is assisted by Andrès Vargas during walks and overnight camps. Enrique founded the tourism project in 1993 using his knowledge from previous employment in the tourism industry and start-up funds from RICANCIE. Angelika Raimann of AmaZOOnico assisted with the administration and design of the ecotourism complex; however, she is no longer involved.

According to RICANCIE, Runa Huasi received approximately 115 visitors in 1997. In order to accommodate higher numbers, the project plans to rebuild the older *cabañas*, thus increasing their capacity to 14 persons. Presently, groups of 2-12 people are accepted. Contact RICANCIE to arrange a visit. Visitors should bring a mosquito net and rubber boots in case of shortfall.

Map: CT OIV-A2 Puerto Misahuallí

CAPIRONA (RICANCIE)

Known around the world as one of the first CBE programs anywhere (Colvin 1994, Wesche 1993, 1995, Izko 1995), Capirona is as reliable and well-rooted as the tree it is named after. A short drive and a hike from Tena, Capirona has exceptional lodgings and a cultural presentation that is not to be missed. Relative to the other RICANCIE communities, Capirona's trails are easy and well defined, thus are most suitable for first time hikers and families.

Every stay in the Capirona community includes a cultural presentation of song, dance and the making of Quichua handicrafts performed in a theater built solely for that purpose. Keep in mind that this is an intercultural exchange where visitors are also asked to present their own culture in song, dance or story! The ecotourism program includes easy jungle walks to giant *ceibo* and colorful *capirona* trees, a birders' look-out spot, and a salt lick cavern, called the Saladero de Aicha Llahuana, for viewing nocturnal creatures. Intermixed with these activities are hours of free time where tourists can swim in the Río Puni, play volleyball, tan on the beach, explore the surrounding paths, or read up on Quichua history. Depending upon when you visit, you may get the chance to participate in a community work project. Every visit to Capirona includes a tour of the community center including the school houses, the chapel and the soccer field. Samples of *chicha*, a traditional staple in the Quichua diet, can be tasted here too. All of these program components can be spread over a three to six-night time period upon request.

Capirona is a community owned ecotourism program which rotates the project's workers and administrators on a regular basis. The four RICANCIE-trained guides, namely Cristóbal Vargas (head guide), Samuel Tapuy, Otavio Alvarado and Cesario Andy manage visitor activities, interactions with the community and special requests. Capirona will continue to invest in its human resources by arranging for additional guiding courses and supplementary training for those already involved in ecotourism.

This CBE program was established in 1990 to discourage the intrusion of oil development. Since then the operation has expanded, not only into a more effective means of ensuring autonomy of indigenous territory, but also as a template for other ecotourism initiatives. The Fundación Jatun Sacha, located on the banks of the Río Napo east of the community, sends students to learn about the Capirona example and appreciate how tourism can be used to protect nature and indigenous culture.

Capirona's territory covers 2 000 hectares of land of which three quarters is intact primary forest, the remainder being reserved by the community for agricultural purposes. Upon exploration of the banks of the Río Puni, one will find 70 Capirona families dispersed in both directions from the community center near which the ecotourism complex is located. There are three sleeping *cabañas* at this ecotourism site; two of these also boast flush toilets and showers. Another much more rustic *cabaña*, located 45 minutes away by foot, on the Río Rumi Yacu, is used upon request for those who wish to experience a more adventurous night in the jungle. The community plans to renovate this building, thus transforming it into a fully equipped *cabaña* in the near future. The main tourism complex also includes a store (where pop and handicrafts can be purchased), a kitchen/dining *cabaña*, a theater, a volleyball court, a beach, a two-way radio, a well, latrines, two large motor canoes, two dugout paddle canoes, and several well maintained walking trails.

For arrangements, tourists must contact the RICANCIE office, preferably a month in advance, especially during the busy season, since Capirona is the most frequently visited community of the RICANCIE network. Unannounced visitors are not accepted. Guests meet their guide at the RICANCIE office from where a public bus (a one-hour ride) takes you to the trailhead where the trip continues by foot (for two hours). If the Río Puni is high, there is the potential of going in and out by canoe from Ahuano.

Map: CT OIV-A2 Puerto Misahuallí

SALAZAR AITACA (RICANCIE)

Fit and adventurous tourists will want to "attacka" Aitaca. The terrain is physically demanding so get ready to slip, slide, climb and scramble, and don't be surprised if you get stuck in the mud! It is the site of numerous water pools, where one can swim and fish, and observe spectacular waterfalls, including one which plunges 80 meters downstream from a secluded lagoon - a very picturesque area. Natural wonders include a semi-open cave which houses oil birds, and which is only a short (but slippery) climb away from historical petroglyphs. If you are willing to endure the routine - hike, play, explore, eat and sleep - this tour will be well worth the effort! The tourist will always be rewarded with the raw beauty of nature and a breathtaking scenery at the end of every trail.

Named after its founder, Salazar Aitaca was established approximately 80 years ago. A CBE project was established in 1994. Since then, Aitaca has received only 18 tourist groups of three to six people; nine tourists visited during 1997. The eco-tourism territory of Aitaca is owned by Carlos Alvarado, a member, although the ecotourism program and infrastructure are communally-owned. The project is run by 18 community members who work on a rotational system. Aitaca has community work days every three months which involve lots of *chicha*! (fresh in the morning and fermented at night!). At the time of writing, the community was working on the new *cabaña* complex which it hoped to complete by September 1998. With good timing, tourists can observe and possibly participate in one of these work parties.

The numerous rivers and streams that originate in the area make Aitaca a major contributor to the Río Misahuallí (and a natural water park!). The community and *cabañas* are located deep inside the primary forest and are surrounded by secondary forest.

Besides the beauty of the physical environment, natural attractions include abnormally large and colorful insects (10 inch moths!), poison arrow frogs, reptiles, and large snails which are a gastronomic treat for the Quichua! Wild animals include monkeys, peccaries, and ocelots. The community *shaman* may be visited for a general presentation or for a personal purification ceremony. Nearby petroglyphs mark the *shaman's* sacred area.

Programs vary and average tourist visits are between two and five days. A minimum of three people is required. Cave and petroglyph visits make for a half-day venture, while the hikes to the lagoon and waterfalls each take the better part of a day. All hikes include explanations of the flora and fauna by your guides, José and Olmeda Salazar and Luis Yumbo. At the end of a busy and exciting day, tourists can relax under the small, therapeutic cascades at the foot of the *cabañas*. Wet and dry seasons, (May/June, and December respectively), affect the depth and power of streams and pools, so check water levels before plunging in.

The community has begun to expand its facilities in order to accommodate up to 12 tourists. The new *cabaña* will include a shared bathroom, and a larger cooking and dining area. Purified running water, a septic system, and electricity will be installed in the future. There are also plans to add a botanical and medicinal garden near the *cabaña*. A foot bridge across the Río Misahuallí, linking Aitaca to the ecotourism program of Machacuyacu (see "Machacuyacu"), is under construction. The bridge will be constructed during community work days and completion is anticipated for June 1999, although this depends on the availability of outside funds.

There will also be a new program which proposes some night ventures: an overnight in old *cabañas* at the lagoon and an evening hike to experience the tropical night life! Camping is possible along the trail to the Río Misahuallí and an overnight stay at Machacuyacu is also a future possibility. The new cultural program will include trapping demonstrations, and a traditional mock wedding ceremony.

You can count on two hours to enter the community under dry conditions; one hour by road transport from Tena (provided by RICANCIE) and one hour to hike to the *cabañas*, which are situated between two mountains on the north side of the Río Misahuallí. The hike is a combination of a muddy colonist cow path, which narrows onto the community's paths, and log-laid trails. Overall, the hiking is challenging for fit individuals, so pack lightly to ease the trip.

Aitaca is a nature lover's playground, so be creative and adventurous. The scenic and wildlife photo opportunities are endless! Unfortunately, the terrain is steep and can get quite slippery and muddy, but in the end, hard work is always rewarded!

Map: CT OIII-E4 Lushanta

RÍO BLANCO (RICANCIE)

Río Blanco is best known for its *shaman* and healer Augustin Grefa, and the extensive medicinal plant garden he meticulously keeps. Augustin also works as the main guide, and has played a major part in establishing this well-run CBE enterprise. Located north of the Río Napo, between Puerto Misahuallí and Ahuano, its program is one of the better established of the RICANCIE network. The Río Guambuno borders the main complex which is surrounded by secondary forest. More extensive programs are available for the adventurous and fit traveler who would like to camp under the stars and enjoy extensive forest hikes in the Cordillera Galeras further north (Map 4).

The serene atmosphere at the *cabaña* complex is due to its ideal location in a secluded and tranquil setting, a 20-minute walk from the community. Four small *cabañas* and a communal dormitory can accomodate up to 25 people. A kitchen, a dining *cabaña* and central bathrooms with flush toilet and shower complete the simple but comfortable infrastructure.

The standard four-day program at Río Blanco includes day hikes, cultural presentations, participation in a communal work day and viewing of local handicrafts. Two or five-day programs are also available for those with more or less time on their hands. An extensive garden with over 410 plant species is used for teaching purposes. Augustin knows these plants well and puts much effort into ensuring that this knowledge is passed on to the younger generation. He accompanies tourists to magnificent bathing cascades and on pleasant forest walks where he gives detailed explanations of plants and their healing virtues and uses.

The more adventurous camping enthusiast will enjoy a four to five-day trek to the outlying Galeras Reserve. Renown for its wildlife, lagoons and majestic vistas, excursions to this area can be arranged with the local guide. Unless you intend to undertake the more challenging trip, where camping equipment is required, it is strongly recommended to pack as lightly as possible.

From Tena, tourists take a one-hour bus or taxi ride to Ahuano, then a 15-minute canoe ride across the Río Napo to the trailhead. From here it is a moderately strenuous, two-hour uphill hike to Río Blanco. Alternatively, you can also access the trailhead by canoe from Misahuallí.

Group sizes may vary between two and 25 persons, and spontaneous arrivals are not advised. The best time to visit this area is May through August, which is also the peak tourist season.

The ecotourism facilities are run rotationally by 36 community members. Río Blanco has been operating its ecotourism project since 1994 and plans to completely renovate the existing infrastructure over the summer of 1998. Interested tourists can contact the community through RICANCIE's office in Tena, where you will also meet your guide.

Maps: CT OIV-A2 Puerto Misahuallí; CT OIII-E4 Lushanta

CHUVA URCU (RICANCIE)

The family-run program of Chuva Urcu offers tourism facilities lending access to a 13 000 hectare communally-owned reserve located south of Ahuano on the Río Gusano. Chuva Urcu will bring out the explorer in all of its guests as they clamber over the creeks, rivers and gullies that slice throughout the territory, or take the overnight, 10-kilometer trek up and along the 650-meter high ridge of Chuva Urcu Mountain.

The tourist complex is located on the Río Gusano, a small tributary of the Río Arajuno. The community's land consists of mostly primary forest drained by a network of streams which have created many steep and narrow valleys. The reserve is bounded by Huaorani territory to the south and by colonists on all other sides. Chuva Urcu's 25 families also operate *chacras* within this territory, yet are not permanently settled in the area; therefore the majority of their territory has felt little human impact.

Sleeping *cabañas* overlooking the Río Gusano provide accommodations for six persons in private rooms. Washroom facilities with a shower and running water are located close by. An open-air dining room has recently been added where filling, traditional dishes are served. Built of local materials, this new structure displays the fine craftsmanship of its builders and provides a relaxed and easygoing atmosphere for journal writing and candlelit chats in the evening. In the works, are rooms with double beds at the main complex as well as a six-person sleeping *cabaña* located one hour up the Río Gusano.

Stays at the *cabañas* are three to five days in length with the focus of any visit being on the strenuous, six-hour overnight hike to the summit ridge of Chuva Urcu Mountain. Liana swinging

(Tarzan style) and swimming keep hikers entertained along the way. The look-out at the end of the walk offers expansive views of the Napo Valley, the town of Ahuano and the Cordillera Galeras to the northeast. Other natural attractions include unexplored caves, beautiful streams and rivers for swimming, snorkeling and riverbed hiking, with at least three giant *ceibo* trees within minutes of the *cabaña* complex. As well, numerous hunting trails provide an opportunity for strenuous hiking in case Chuva Urcu Mountain does not satisfy your cravings! More leisurely attractions such as basket weaving demonstrations, fish-trap construction and gold panning are offered in your spare time. Opportunities for spear fishing of catfish exist for those with good hand-eye coordination and an appetite for fresh fish.

Although a RICANCIE member since 1994, poor administration has thrust responsibility for the program at Chuva Urcu onto the Cerda family's shoulders. The 40 visitors that have arrived in 1998 have been fed by Cecilia's gifted cooking, while her husband Carlos has handled all of the jungle excursions. A second guide is presently studying in Quito. Arrangements to visit the community are made through RICANCIE's office. Groups of three to six persons are preferred and at least one day's notice is required. Access to and from Tena is via the road to the bridge over the Río Arajuno at Campococha (Map4). At the bridge, a motorized canoe is hired for the 20-minute ride upriver to the trailhead. From there, a one-hour hike on a fairly good trail brings you to the cabaña complex on the Río Gusano. In the future, exit from the community may be by dugout paddle canoe down the Gusano, but at the present time no canoes are available. Light packs are essential for the long hikes you will take. This should be easy to achieve as sleeping gear is provided; however, it may be a good idea to bring a water purifier or tablets along for your group. The required fitness level for this program is high as all the hikes are strenuous.

Maps: CT OIV-A2 Puerto Misahuallí; CT OIV-A4 Arajuno

LAS GALERAS (RICANCIE)

Tucked away on the southern bank of the Río Guambuno, the RICANCIE community of Las Galeras has a taste of everything for the avid tourist seeking adventure, spectacular mountain views and an eye-opening cultural experience. The Cordillera Galeras which rises in the distance adds to the scenic setting and offers a physically demanding hike to a mountain look-out. The ease of interaction between tourists and the community members makes for an intimate intercultural exchange.

The community consists of some 280 inhabitants who practice subsistence farming on small agricultural plots sprinkled throughout the valley and along the river. The area offers a diversity of landscape and topography, from the rushing rivers and plunging waterfalls above to the primary and secondary forest that carpet the valley walls and floor.

The inhabitants of Las Galeras are hospitable, charming and enthusiastic about sharing their knowledge and lifestyle with their guests. Cultural attractions include a handicraft demonstration, preparation of typical Quichua food, explanation of medicinal plant use, the possibility of learning about shamanism, and a traditional farewell ceremony (*despedida*) on the final night. On the natural side, this semi-secluded area offers strenuous jungle hikes through secondary and primary rainforest in and around Sumaco-Galeras National Park. A full day hike brings one to the spectacular look-out where an overnight camping site is prepared by members of the community. Weather permitting, it is strongly recommended to awaken before daybreak at this look-out in order to marvel at the sun as it rises over the greens of the jungle in the valley below. Further trekking brings one to several isolated waterfalls and to a cave which, according to the locals, contains "shamanic" spirits. Other activities include swimming in invigorating freshwater rivers, dugout canoe paddling and fishing in the picturesque Río Guambuno.

At present, Las Galeras offers fixed programs for three to five-day stays with much room for flexibility. It is also possible to make day-visits to the nearby communities of Río Blanco (see Río Blanco) and San Pedro, to participate in a local community work day, or to try your hand at gold panning. One factor that may significantly alter the basic tourist program is seasonality. Water levels are highest during the months of May through June and at times may impede crossing the Río Guambuno, even via canoe. On these rare occasions, programs are confined to the community and surrounding areas. However, keep in mind that with high water levels come more spectacular waterfalls.

The CBE enterprise was founded in 1994. Two RICANCIE-trained guides coordinate the operation along with several other associates. Francisco Ayuinda, the main guide, will captivate you with his detailed knowledge and awareness of the Ecuadorian flora and fauna, especially concerning medicinal plants (the small medicinal garden is well worth a visit). Community members are supportive of the ecotourism project and are eager to interact with visitors. They readily take part in the handicraft demonstration and encourage tourist participation in the music and dance performance.

The ecotourism project has received a limited number of tourists due to the lack of marketing. Nonetheless, its overall organization and infrastructure clearly indicate the potential for increased inflow. The Quichua-style *cabañas* are situated just outside the community center, within easy walking distance of the rainforest. The site boasts two clean and well-maintained *cabañas*. These comfortably accommodate up to six visitors, with room for an additional six in the local health center or in outdoor tents. With increased demand, the community envisions improving its infrastructure to include surplus sleeping quarters and a small cultural museum.

Las Galeras is reached via Río Blanco (see Río Blanco). You first make your way by road to Punta Ahuano (one hour). Once there, your guide will arrange to transport you 15 minutes upriver to Puerto Misicocha. From the trailhead, a two and a half-hour hike (mostly uphill) through Río Blanco will bring you to the community's *cabañas*. Depending on water levels, a dugout paddle canoe may transport you between the community of Río Blanco and Las Galeras. Pack lightly !

Maps: CT OIV-A2 Puerto Misahuallí; CT OIII-E4 Lushanta

SAN JOSE DE PUMA PUNGO (RICANCIE)

If you have traveled overland through Ecuador's jungles and rivers, why not consider heading underground in San José de Puma Pungo? Speleology enthusiasts, both novice and expert, will be fascinated by this area's vast network of caves that can be explored on one's own, or, as a guided tour. This CBE program is currently being planned by the Women's Association of San José, a community east of Archidona, and will eventually be part of the RICANCIE network. All facilities will be constructed on community work days and members who will be involved with services will operate on a rotational basis.

San José controls a small, 130-hectare reserve, which has been designated as the site of its future ecotourism complex. This reserve is located north of, and is accessed via Puerto Misahuallí (Map 4). Despite its small size and surrounding colonized lands, the site has remained largely intact and is ideal for tourism. In addition to the network of underground caves, the area comprises 30-meter waterfalls, lagoons and impressive scenery.

A traditional Quichua-style complex is to be built in proximity of these main attractions, at the entrance of the reserve. Two *cabañas* will serve as sleeping accommodations for up to 10 persons, while a third will serve as a kitchen/dining *cabaña*. A septic tank will also be added along with flush toilets and showers. The site is adjacent to a major cave mouth, within five minutes of the waterfalls, and could quickly be explored within a day's time.

The caving experience will be appropriate for everyone, from first-timers accompanied by trained guides to experts wishing to poke their noses in unexplored caverns on their own. Tourists may also stay overnight in the caves - but beware of bats and catnapping pumas! Basic equipment will be available such as rubber boots, flashlights and helmets. Those wishing to go beyond a casual cave visit should bring their own gear. Caving in the Ecuadorian Amazon is also subject to the weather. The sporadic and intense rainfalls that characterize the Oriente cause water levels to rise suddenly, thus limiting the accessibility of the caves and creating some risk. Visits during the dry season (November to February) should yield longer and more frequent opportunities underground.

Other activities will include hiking throughout the area and drifting down the Río Misahuallí on a balsa wood raft. Presently, there are four well established trails for hiking, and discussions into the possibility of expanding this trail network to the Copayacu River are proceeding well. Once this extension is completed, the program will be connected to the RICANCIE communities of Salazar Aitaca and Machacuyacu (Map 4).

Tourists are also invited to visit the community (located east of Archidona), which is rather unique as it is actively managed by women. A visit would not be complete without experiencing this distinct community arrangement. Their cultural program will undoubtedly reflect women's involvement through typical theatrical dances, tours of botanical gardens and ceramic expositions.

San José de Puma Pungo can be accessed by foot from Pununo, north of Puerto Misahuallí. It is a moderate two-hour walk along a colonist trail. Along the way, visitors cross over the Río Pisuno via a covered footbridge and gradually follow a scenic trail into elevated grounds. The trail follows the Río Misahuallí for a good part of the way and offers impressive views of the Río Napo valley. Eventually, the site will also be accessible via a four-hour hike from Salazar Aitaca, once the trail is established.

Five to 10 tourists can be accommodated.

Price: Undetermined; likely to be similar to RICANCIE communities.

Contact: See RICANCIE

Map: CT OIII-E3 Tena; CT OIV-A2 Puerto Misahuallí

HUACAMAYOS

The Huacamayos region consists of 11 Quichua communities located at the foot of the Huacamayos mountain range (Map 4) which have formed the "Union of Communities for the Use and Management of Natural Resources of the Huacamayos" in order to ensure better living conditions for their people. Improved living standards are, in their view, best promoted by communal management centered on social welfare and environmental protection. Emphasis has been put on the protection of the region's rare natural biodiversity, its rich ancestral culture and the economic well-being of the locals. Each of the 11 communities has developed a small-scale sustainable project which is jointly managed by the community and the Union. The main activities include agroforestry, intercropping, medicinal plant gardens, herbal essences and ecotourism, all of which are important for the economic independence of the indigenous people of Huacamayos. This association is proud to have established one central CBE program in the community of AACLLAC which fits perfectly into the communities' ideology and has proven to be a profitable enterprise. AACLLAC also serves as the coordination centre of the other communities' tourism programs.

The Huacamayos mountain range, centerpiece of the Huacamayos Union, is the final major ridge of the eastern slope of the Andes. There exists a natural division between the western and eastern halves of this range. The western part, bordered by the Río Chalupas, has more accentuated topography and is dominated by high-altitude montane forest. Its main feature is the deep, uninhabited and luxuriant Verdeyacu valley. The eastern part is characterised by more moderate slopes where settlement and agriculture flourish. Colonization has occurred mainly along the Tena-Jondachi-Baeza road which is the eastern limit of the region. This road provides easy access from Tena. The Huacamayos is the heart of the Quichua nationality and the ancient spiritual ties with the forest are visible through numerous petroglyphs found throughout the area.

AACLLAC (HUACAMAYOS)

The community of AACLLAC, located on the banks of the Río Tena, serves as the ecotourism staging center for the Huacamayos region, and at the time of writing was the only community fully equipped to accommodate tourists in comfort. Despite its proximity to Tena, this peaceful haven provides exceptional tranquility. It also offers excellent cuisine as well as an exciting range of activities. Day and overnight trips to the Huacamayos communities listed below can easily be arranged from here, exposing the tourist to a variety of attractions including petroglyphs, caves, waterfalls, hot springs, healing waters, pottery workshops, medicinal plant gardens and shamanic rituals.

Since July of 1997, an average of 12 tourists per month have visited AACLLAC. The community regularly offers five-day packages including lodging and three daily meals, but will also accommodate special requests. Quichua dances, pottery work and medicinal plant use comprise the main cultural attractions. Educational forest excursions with native guides, water activities such as inner tubing and canoeing, and playing sports with the locals will keep the tourist in shape. An elaborate medicinal plant garden at the heart of the ecotourism complex is the pride of the community. Relaxing activities include a visit to AACLLAC's fish farm (*piscicultura*), walking on moderate trails through primary forest, and enjoying a panoramic view of the Cordillera Huacamayos from a comfortable hammock. In addition, day trips to the outlying communities can be combined with a stay at the AACLLAC ecotourism complex. When planning day trips, take into account that sporadic weather patterns, ranging from glaring sun to strong downpours, can dramatically affect river levels and access to surrounding communities. Prices are very affordable, considering the high quality of the accommodations, the warm hospitality of the staff and the delicious, locally prepared meals.

Tourism operations are extremely well organized and carried out. This is exemplified by the special attention to detail which is present in everything from the elaborate traditional meals to the sturdily designed accommodations. The *cabañas* are clustered in a central public area surrounded by agricultural lands, and bordered by the Río Tena. Built in traditional fashion, three well-maintained thatched roof structures make up the sleeping quarters with capacity for 16 individuals. Double, triple and communal rooms are available. These guarded huts are furnished with electricity, comfortable beds, clean bedding and mosquito nets. Three individual washrooms with showers, flush toilets and running water are located outside the dormitories.

For the members of AACLLAC, ecotourism represents an incentive to preserve traditional knowledge while promoting environmental awareness. Experienced and knowledgeable native guides lead tourists through program activities. Work is done on a rotational basis involving the participation of all 38 community members. Various tasks such as cooking, maintenance, guiding and security are provided by competent and friendly community members.

AACLLAC is located a 15-minute taxi ride from Tena (or an easy 45-minute walk). Tourists pay for their transportation during visits to AACLLAC and the other 10 Huacamayos communities but taxi rental is arranged by AACLLAC. To visit this CBE project, it is best to leave a message five days in advance with Benito Nantipa, although spontaneous arrivals can be accommodated.

Prices: $31 to $35/person/day package (depending on group size); selected services are available at lower prices.

Contact: Benito Nantipa, Presidente "Unión Huacamayos", c/o Federación de Organizaciones Indígenas del Napo (FOIN), Calle Augusto Rueda 242, Casilla Postal 217, Tena, Napo, tel: (06) 886 288

Tropic Ecological Adventures, Av. República 307 y Almagro, Edif. Taurus, Dpto. 1-A, Quito, tel.: (593 2) 225 907, 234 594, fax: (5932) 560 756, e-mail: tropic@uio.satnet.net, www.tropiceco.com

Maps: CT ÑIII-F2 Antisana; CT ÑIII-F4 Chalupas; CT OIII-E1Sardinas; CT OIII-E3 Tena

SHAMATO-SARDINAS (HUACAMAYOS)

The Shamato community borders the Antisana Ecological Reserve in the northernmost part of the Huacamayos region. A two-day trip from AACLLAC is necessary in order to combine the variety of activities offered in the Shamato area. Surrounded by pristine wilderness, an impressive network of caves draped with lush vegetation and interlaced with streams of clear healing water can be explored at one's leisure. Visitors will also enjoy bathing in a 30-meter cascade, visiting a medicinal plant garden and hiking through dense primary cloud forest. Proper footwear with good ankle support is necessary for the challenging hikes to these attractions, and on to the simple communal *cabaña*. Guests should bring their own sleeping bag, mat and mosquito net. A medium to high fitness level is required as the trails are rugged and located on harsh terrain.

The Shamato trailhead is at kilometer 18 of the Tena-Baeza road, near the settlement of Sardinas. On the return trip to AACLLAC you will walk through Sardinas and stop at the historic Anaconda petroglyph, the symbol for the Huacamayos Union.

SAN FRANCISCO (HUACAMAYOS)

The community of San Francisco offers a two-day hike including visits to cascades, caves and lagoons at the head of the Río Calmito Yacu. Various petroglyphs can be encountered in the area surrounding San Francisco and its neighboring community, 20 de Mayo. San Francisco is easily accessed within a half-hour by taxi from AACLLAC.

SANTA RITA (HUACAMAYOS)

Tourists can visit Santa Rita as a day trip from AACLLAC. Just north of Archidona, this community offers a pottery workshop and well-preserved petroglyphs as its main attractions. The former consists of a traditional studio which also serves as a pottery school. Tourists are invited to try their hand at molding clay under the instruction of community elders. Quichua pottery made in the community is also for sale.

A short walk from the handicraft complex are two impressive rocks with ancient petroglyphs representing the male and the female. Their hilltop location overlooks the village, providing a spectacular view of the mountainous landscape. Trails lead through the surrounding primary forest where 18 species of palm trees can be examined. A somewhat rough half-hour taxi ride west from Tena brings you to the community.

ATACAPI (HUACAMAYOS)

Bordered by the Río Tena, Atacapi is within close proximity of the Chiuta Mountain, an important historical site. The community offers a moderate day hike to a breathtaking look-out overlooking the Tena region. Various Quichua ceramics can be purchased in Atacapi, and there remains the possibility of an impromptu cultural performance if you're lucky. The community is located approximately 25 minutes from Tena by road.

ALTO TENA (HUACAMAYOS)

Alto Tena is located at the foot of the Cordillera Huacamayos, surrounded by dense vegetation. This small Quichua community can be reached by a moderate two-hour hike from Atacapi where the road peters out. From the village center, a further 45-minute hike along the Río Pashimbi brings you to a beautiful 30-meter waterfall.

MUSEO AMAZONICO (HUACAMAYOS)

Located approximately 15 minutes north of Tena in the town of Archidona, this museum is well identified by a large sign on the main road. A massive boulder with petroglyphs lies at the entrance, surrounded by a medicinal plant garden. An impressive interpretative center features displays on the different indigenous groups found in the Ecuadorian Amazon. Brief descriptions of each ethnic community with artifacts, audio-visual presentations, and native interpreters provide the tourists with a complete overview of native Amazonian culture. Typical food, grown on site, can be sampled to complete the experience.

SAPOLLO

A group of very enthusiastic residents of this Quichua village, situated southwest of Tena, have been putting great effort into restarting their ecotourism program. Sapollo is the only CBE program operating on the Río Jatunyacu (Map 4). With its easily accessible location and fairly low cost, it is ideally suited for tourists with an interest in agriculture. Other attractions include the petroglyphs located on either side of the hanging footbridge which connects Bajo Talag with Sapollo, and the manual *tarabita* (cable car) which you can ride across the Río Jatunyacu upriver from Sapollo, providing a good arm workout for those who are not afraid of heights!

Increasing pressure for land is one of the reasons that Sapollo, primarily an agricultural community, has turned to ecotourism to diversify its economy. The community's 150 hectare property extends three kilometers south from the river. The rear two kilometers consist of forested, non-cultivable highlands which are to be used for tourism. In May 1998, the community received a government grant to improve its tourism infrastructure. With the help of Fundación Ayuda en Acción, an Ecuadorian NGO, community members have been busy with the construction and planning of their program. Once established, they hope to re-associate themselves to the RICANCIE network, with whom they previously worked. How the entire community will be involved in the program is not yet fully determined, but profits from ecotourism will be shared with the entire community. Guiding expertise will be provided by Silverio Andy Vargas and Luis Pablo Andy Vargas.

At the moment, the community can accommodate eight guests in four recently built sleeping *cabañas*. The complex also includes a dining hall and bathrooms to which showers will soon be added. Well water is available on site. The facilities are all located a short walk from the Jatunyacu River and are surrounded by secondary forest and fields of *yuca* and banana belonging to the community.

Sapollo plans to offer a mixed culture-nature tourism program. Cultural activities will include traditional food preparation, music, dancing, a shamanic presentation and a farewell ceremony on the last day of your stay. Natural attractions include a one-hour walk to the south where intact forest and the headwaters of the Río Pioculin lie on higher ground. This excursion brings you to a look-out, and to a river spot where guests can swim and pan for gold. The community plans to rebuild a *cabaña* that previously existed at this location, but in the interim you can arrange to camp instead. Wildlife enthusiasts may want to visit Sapollo's 150 hectare forest reserve located between the Ríos Pibi and Ila, accessible by a four to six-hour hike. Such a trip requires overnight camping, thus necessitating supplementary planning with your guides.

Access to the area is by bus or taxi from Tena (one hour) to the foot bridge at Bajo Talag. From there, a 20-minute walk on a flat trail along the south side of the Jatunyacu brings you to Sapollo. Costs are among the lowest in the area at 25$ to 30$ per day including food and accommodation. If for no other reason, this community should be visited for its dedication to making this CBE project succeed!

Price: $25 to $30/person/day.

Contact: Samuel Shiguango, Fundación Ayuda en Acción, Av. Juan Leon Mera 647, Tena, Napo, tel: 886 614, telefax: 887 254

Map: CT-OIV-A1 PuertoNapo

X
COMMUNITY BASED ECOTOURISM IN PASTAZA

The province of Pastaza is distinct from the previously discussed regions since the vast majority of its area is covered by an uninterrupted block of indigenous territories (Map 5). The Quichua control the core of this block, while the Huaorani, Záparo, Shiwiar, Achuar and Shuar territories constitute its peripheries. The majority of this territory was awarded as a result of the dramatic march of Pastaza *indígenas* to Quito in 1992, led by OPIP. This block of indigenous territories is strategically located, preventing overland access to the southern part of Yasuní National Park as well as the unoccupied National Security Zone along the Peruvian boundary. Thus the totality of the Pastaza lowlands are, in effect, an indigenous controlled nature reserve with some small islands of indigenous land use. OPIP's vision is to protect this block of native lands by promoting the concept of an indigenous Biosphere Reserve (Cerda 1998).

Only the small *selva alta* portion in the west of Pastaza has been strongly affected by settler agriculture. Puyo is the main urban center of this area and is the capital of Pastaza province. With a population of over 20 000, it is the best equipped town in the Oriente. Puyo is the transportation hub of the area with major roads north to Tena, west to Baños and Ambato in the highlands, and south to Macas. The eastern lowlands of Pastaza can only be reached by chartered single engine airplane and canoe, which together offer the opportunity to visit very remote parts of the Ecuadorian Amazon.

CBE ventures in Pastaza province are small and relatively new. Potential tourists have a wide range of choices, from one or even half-day visits near Puyo to rugged, multi-day, fly-in river trips deep into the untouched jungle.

ATACAPI TOURS

ATACAPI Tours is OPIP's semi-independent ecotourism agency through which the organization hopes to promote CBE and environmental conservation. It is operated under contract with the Quichua family-owned Papangu Tours. Its office is in the center of Puyo next to the well-stocked indigenous handicraft store Yana Puma, also a dependency of OPIP.

ATACAPI Tours was initially established in 1994 with the support of DED, a German development organization. Ecotourism coordinator and guide training courses were organized and managed by Acción Amazonía. The enterprise collapsed in 1996 as the result of mismanagement and political scandals involving OPIP leaders associated with the Bucaram government. OPIP learned its lesson. It restructured ATACAPI Tours from a political dependency into a largely autonomous commercial enterprise, again with DED support.

This restructuring is now complete, and ATACAPI Tours is in the process of re-establishing its links with CBE communities which had been alienated by the preceding fracas. ATACAPI Tours is developing a wide range of programs from day visits to multi-day canoe trips and fly-in adventures. Given OPIP's control of most of the forest lands of Pastaza, there is abundant scope for further CBE development once effective marketing has been established.

Contact: ATACAPI Tours
Programa de Ecoturismo de la OPIP
9 de Octubre y Atahualpa
Antiguo Municipio
Segundo Piso
Puyo, Pastaza
telefax (03) 883 875

ETHNOBOTANICAL PARK OMAERE
(ATACAPI TOURS)

This beautiful ethnobotanical park, run in collaboration with OPIP and ATACAPI Tours, is located an easy 20-minute walk from the downtown core of Puyo. It makes for an excellent afternoon stop if you have little time to spend in the area. If you'd like a taste of the night jungle, OMAERE Park (Parque OMAERE) also offers an exciting and unique overnight lodging option.

Access to the park is by footbridge over the Río Puyo which seperates it from the city. Clearly marked paths wind through the park, taking you through an aquatic garden, demonstration *chacras*, an orchidarium, a hummingbird garden, and various typical indigenous dwellings. If you wish to spend the night, a pleasant tourist complex with capacity for 15 persons amongst trees stands near the main entrance, almost within view of downtown Puyo. Built in traditional style with a thatched roof and a wooden structure, the sleeping *cabaña* is furnished with beds, sheets, and mosquito nets. The building complex includes fully equipped washrooms, offices, meeting rooms and a handicraft store. Visitors can camp on park grounds.

The project's objective is to educate tourists about the sensitive rainforest ecosystem, to inform school children about their natural and cultural heritage, and to teach indigenous people about sustainable development and alternative forms of agriculture. Self-guided walks with an information pamphlet are the norm; however, visitors may try to arrange guided tours with the friendly staff.

To get to Parque OMAERE, follow Avenida 9 de Octubre north from downtown Puyo to the footbridge over the Río Puyo. As the following address suggests, you can swim in the river.

Price: $2 entrance fee; $5 for lodging; $3 for camping.
Contact: Carlos Piruchkun - Administrador, Parque Pedagógico Etnobotánico OMAERE, Paseo Turístico, El Balneario, Casilla 770, Puyo, Pastaza; telefax (593 3) 883 001,
e-mail: parque@omaere2.ecuanex.net.ec

FÁTIMA - INDI CHURIS - HOLA VIDA
(**ATACAPI** Tours)

This combined program, offered by ATACAPI Tours, involves visiting the Fátima animal preserve, the Quichua community of Indi Churis, and the ecological project of Hola Vida. Due to their proximity to Puyo, these attractions are easily accessible. This full day trip, ideal for groups of five or more, provides tourists with an introduction to a variety of natural attractions including tropical jungle wildlife, an impressive cascade in primary forest, and beautiful vistas from a look-out. A Spanish-speaking guide will accompany you.

From Puyo, a 15-minute drive north on the Tena road brings you to Fátima. This OPIP-supported animal project provides protection for species native to the region. During a short, easy stroll through a small petting zoo area with walk-in cages, visitors are introduced to typical fauna including tapirs, aquatic turtles, *capivaras,* lizards, alligators, macaws, parrots and snakes, among others. The Quichua manager is more than happy to spend time answering questions and talking about animal habitat preservation and the development of the 150 hectare preserve which contains further wildlife in a natural setting. Check out their small library for detailed information on tropical flora and fauna.

From Fátima, one drives 45 minutes south through Puyo to the small community of Indi Churis, perched on a hillock overlooking the junction of the Ríos Puyo and Pastaza. Here, lunch is served in a typical cabaña. After a brief look around and a participatory blowgun demonstration you will leave to explore the Hola Vida territory, a mixed conservation-ecotourism project developed by the Indi Churis community with help from OPIP. An easy three-hour walk through magnificent primary rainforest brings you first to an impressive look-out over Pastaza's plains, thick with vegetation and enhanced by picturesque rivers. Continuing through the jungle, the trail ends at a virtual paradise with the 30-meter high Hola Vida waterfall where tourists can rest and swim.

This program is also available as a two-day trip with an overnight in Indi Churis. At present the *cabaña* facilities in the community are somewhat run down; thus, as the full program can easily be completed in one day, we recommend the shorter tour until the *cabañas* are reconstructed. A planned tourism circuit including the community of San Pedro should soon be available, offering more varied natural and cultural attractions.

All three sites are easily accessed by taxi and each is within 25 minutes of downtown Puyo. An entrance fee of $1 per person is charged at the waterfall; profits go to the community fund.

Price: $28 to $42/person (depending on group size).

SAN PEDRO (ATACAPI Tours)

Of the Pastaza region communities, San Pedro (Map 5) offers the easiest accessibility from Puyo, sturdy lodgings and some spectacular vistas of primary forest and developed lands. Its ecotourism program is a sociologist's dream, showing a startling division between developed and natural spaces. Friendly guides and arranged "meet the people" sessions make the walk to San Pedro an eye-opening experience!

The community is located on the southern shore of the Río Puyo, an hour away from downtown Puyo by taxi, or four much more enriching hours by foot. The north of the river is occupied by colonists while Quichua communities dot the southern side. Just over the southern ridge begins seemingly endless primary rainforest, which rolls down to the Río Pastaza and beyond.

The community's tourism facilities include a sleeping *cabaña*, a common area for eating, latrines, and showers with running water. These buildings are all located adjacent to the guides' home overlooking the turbulent Río Puyo. The complex lies between the community centers of San Pedro and Nuevo Mundo at the third suspension bridge where you can cross over from the highway on the north shore. Trails to the plantations follow the valley walls, and stream out in all directions over the ridge to the rainforest.

The two to three–day program begins at the ATACAPI Tours office in Puyo where your guide, Eduardo Vargas, will meet you and lead you to San Pedro. It is highly recommended that you opt to hike rather than drive to the community. The well-maintained foot trail begins by crossing the first suspension bridge at Unión Base, continuing on the north side until it crosses the second bridge at Rosario Yacu (by canoe if the bridge is under repair). From there it continues on the south side of the river to San Pedro. Be prepared for the impact of Puyo's (lack of) waste management on your hike - chances are that if the river has recently been high, refuse will have collected in tree branches and shrubs. Ironically, this makes the ecotourism experience unique and more educational than other operations, especially after seeing the contrast with primary forest later on in the program.

The walk to San Pedro includes visits to area residents to observe their customs (try a bowl of *chicha*!) and their artwork which is sold in the city. Tourists may enjoy listening to tales about life along the Río Puyo. If you are particularly observant, you may see colonist children playing with their indigenous friends from across the divide, demonstrating the harmonious relationship that now exists between the two cultures. This allows the *indígenas* and the settlers to educate their children together, to jointly maintain the trail that you walk in on, and to build suspension bridges that make crossing the tricky Río Puyo much safer.

At the *cabañas*, Eduardo will hand you over to his father Dario, the *shaman* of San Pedro. After you rest from the hike, Dario will welcome you over dinner and introduce you to members of the community. A good night's sleep in beds with blankets, sheets and mosquito nets will leave you fully refreshed for the challenging hike with Dario the following morning. Your guide will point out the medicinal uses of plants in the area in his best Spanish, as he leads you over the steep and hilly terrain (however, he has not mastered the language as well as his son). You are given the not-to-be-missed opportunity to swing on lianas in true jungle style. The vegetation-choked gullies with their small enchanting pools and sunbeams are spectacular for photography.

The highlight of the walk is the look-out just before you head back to the *cabañas*. Fortuitously, a natural landslide has removed the face of a hillside (and all the obscuring trees with it) providing a breathtaking view of the Río Pastaza and the community of Canelos, which contrast sharply with the dirty Río Puyo. The look-out shows the lands of this area as they once were and thankfully still are, in most of Pastaza province.

A unique quality of San Pedro is the food. The family maintains a chicken farm for serving Pollo al Campo. The chickens are a little smelly, but they taste good! An aquaculture project with catfish should be ready shortly, providing an additional source of protein. Tourists are presently required to bring with them the main foods they plan on consuming; however, the family is working on making arrangements for having all culinary necessities brought in or grown on site.

Although there is enough room for nine people in the *cabañas,* at present there is only sufficient sleeping equipment for two. The ideal group size is five or six tourists, enabling you to benefit fully from the skills and knowledge of the guides.

The enterprise is a family operation of Dario, his wife and his son Eduardo, all of whom were involved in the construction of the *cabaña* complex. Funds derived from ecotourism are paid to the family for their services. A Community Foundation fee is also collected which benefits the people of San Pedro in the development of radio communication and other projects. Community leaders of both San Pedro and nearby Nuevo Mundo approve of the enterprise.

Arrange your trip at the ATACAPI Tours office in Puyo a few days in advance so as to send word to San Pedro and advise Eduardo to pick you up. If you plan to walk or drive into the community, please advise the office as well.

Pack lightly and balance your backpack well if you plan to walk in. The trail crosses a number of gullies and there are a few instances where your bridge across consists of a single log (in rubber boots, this can be a little tricky!). The walk to San Pedro will open your eyes to some of the harsh realities of living in this part of the world, as well as show you some of the hidden beauties that lie just over the ridge!

Price: $27 to $38/person/day (depending on group size, 3 day/2 night program).

CHUNCHUPAMBA (ATACAPI Tours)

Overlooking the distant Lomas de Calvario mountains, Chunchupamba is only one and a half hours by car plus two hours by foot southeast of Puyo near the community of Canelos. The physically fit, versatile and patient backpacker will enjoy breathtaking views of primary forest and an enchanting waterfall. One thing is certain, the tourist will feel welcome amongst members of this small, sincere and friendly community.

Crossing through Chunchupamba's 100 hectares of protected area, one can observe the gradual change from cultivated lands to primary forest. The village itself rests on a mountain summit. During this two-hour hike to reach the community three narrow rivers must be crossed by foot, adding to the challenge.

Since a proper *cabaña* complex has not yet been built in the village, tourists initially stay with a local family. Mattresses, pillows and bedding are provided for two people at most - others are relegated to the floor! During the remainder of the program tourists are housed in one of two basic ecotourism *cabañas*. The first is a short hike away in isolated jungle. The other is slightly farther away next to a small lagoon. Each *cabaña* has capacity for eight guests. They are fully equipped, allowing for combined multi-day hiking programs.

Chunchupamba normally offers a three-day program including a variety of activities. The Nalpi waterfall and the Laguna Cuachalala are excellent spots for swimming, fishing and relaxing, while you enjoy the peaceful surroundings. During day-hikes to these locations, your guide will share his limitless knowledge of medicinal plants. At night, guides share the myths and legends of the jungle, regale you with tales of their personal experiences and show off their "war wounds"!

The five families inhabiting Chunchupamba share the responsibilities of greeting tourists, as well as lodging and guiding. Through ATACAPI Tours, tourists pay a contribution to the community to be evenly distributed for medical purposes, education and various other projects. In the future, Chunchupamba plans on building a *cabaña* complex on the outskirts of the community and developing a joint program with Canelos. Since CBE is new to Chunchupamba, small groups of four to five guests are preferred. Mosquito nets, rubber boots, a first-aid kit, food and cooking services are provided; however, given that this is still a new venture, it is suggested that you bring sufficient personal necessities (ex: toilet paper, Power Bars, etc.).

The foot trail to Chunchupamba is easily accessed by taxi from Puyo. Drive south along the Macas road for eight km, then turn left onto Taculin road. A further 18 km drive along a winding gravel road through valleys, cultivated land, and the village of Sanjasilo brings you to the drop-off point. From here, a moderate two-hour hike brings you to the community. Bear in mind that precipitation causes muddy trails which can make for a tougher hike!

Price: $24 to $46/person/day (3day/2night program).

CANELOS – SARAYACU (ATACAPI Tours)

An adventurous, three-day dugout paddle canoe trip brings the tourist from the historic village of Canelos to the community of Sarayacu, one of the most culturally and politically rich Quichua communities of Pastaza, ending with a return flight to Shell by five-seater airplane. A one and a half-hour taxi ride from Puyo to Canelos followed by an hour's hike through the community takes you to the departure point. Here, your three-day canoe journey down the meandering Río Bobonaza begins. While always exciting, the experience depends on the changing river level. It may vary from "sit-back-and-enjoy" to "don't fall overboard into the rushing flood waters"! Along the trajectory, the Bobonaza traverses a hilly landscape, passing several waterfalls and a lagoon.

The first night of the journey is spent in a modest house along the river in proximity to Chapeton. After a second full day in the canoe (six to seven hours), you will most likely (depending on the water level) reach Pacayacu where another basic shelter awaits. A further four hours of downstream travel brings you to the isolated community of Sarayacu on the third day. The final night is spent in the home of a local family, pending completion of an ecotourism complex.

The program in Sarayacu, as it exists presently, allows considerable flexibility. Expect to see the famous Sarayacu pottery, including huge, often *chicha*-filled urns. You will be shown medicinal plants and their use in shamanic practices. If you are lucky, you may be able to attend an unforgettable healing ceremony. Socially-minded tourists will surely appreciate the numerous opportunities to interact directly with the locals. Quality Quichua handicrafts can be purchased in the community and tourists may have their faces painted with traditional designs.

Sarayacu's ecotourism profits are used for communal projects such as the construction of a small bridge, a museum, and a *cabaña* complex. Additionally, funds are allocated for medical treatment and school supplies.

Long reluctant to open itself to outside influences and new to the world of ecotourism, this community of 1 700 inhabitants underwent an extensive discussion process to fully understand the possible impacts of such a venture. As part of the protection of their natural environment and identity, these knowledgeable yet humble people are interested in teaching tourists about different aspects of Quichua culture. They welcome guests into their community as long as group size remains small, and you are as eager to learn from them as they are from you.

As a dramatic end to your journey, a small plane will pick you up during the mid-afternoon on day four for the 20-minute return flight to Shell which shows the contrast between the vast, unbroken canopy of the Quichua territory and the agricultural landscape near Puyo. Be advised that weather is a crucial factor in determining the time of departure. Patience and flexibility are a must!

Food for all meals is purchased by ATACAPI Tours and is included in the package price. In order to ensure a good night's sleep, tourists should bring their own sleeping mat, sleeping bag and mosquito net. As a safety measure, life jackets for the canoe trip are provided. Be prepared for a wet ride; a disposable waterproof camera may be a wise investment. Pack lightly and try not to drink too much *chicha* during your trip, since the five-seater plane holds a maximum of 500 kg!

Price: $31 to $58/person/day (depending on group size, 4day/ 3night program including return flight).

LLANCHAMACOCHA – JANDIAYACU
(ATACAPI Tours)

The two remaining Záparo communities, Llanchamacocha and Jandiayacu, are situated amidst untouched primary rainforest, and are only reachable by light aircraft from Shell. A visit provides a once-in-a-lifetime opportunity to interact with this rapidly disappearing cultural group which is currently being absorbed by the Quichua. The remote surroundings hold a rare biodiversity of fauna amidst unique flora in a breathtaking landscape. This trip is ideally suited for tourists with an interest in ethnobiology; however, adventurous and attentive backpackers will also greatly enjoy the experience, but at a fairly high cost.

Located on the banks of the Río Conambo and in close proximity to the Río Pindoyacu, Llanchamacocha is set in rugged terrain. The neighboring community of Jandiayacu lies a two-day paddle canoe trip downriver. At present, ecotourism is centered in Llanchamacocha; however, the immediate objective is to create a joint program with Jandiayacu which soon hopes to construct its own *cabaña* complex. Together, the two communities have also delimited a reserve wherein hunting and crop cultivation are prohibited. Combined, these two Záparo communities provide ample natural and cultural attractions to appeal to a broad range of tourists.

Both of Llanchamacocha's ecotourism facilities, situated along the Río Conambo, were built in 1996 with the help of ATACAPI Tours. The closest complex, five minutes downriver from the village, is well structured and consists of two sleeping *cabañas* with 15 beds, complete with bedding and mosquito nets. A cooking/dining *cabaña*, a relaxation hut and well equipped bathrooms with showers are within close proximity. A more rustic sleeping *cabaña* at the merging of the Ríos Conambo and Cunguchi lacks equipment; however, this can be transferred from the main complex. It is also possible to sleep in authentic fishing huts along the beach. ATACAPI Tours provides rubber boots, rain ponchos, flashlights and sleeping gear, but you are responsible for all personal items.

Throughout your stay, you will be mesmerized by the beauty of several lagoons, a cascade, abundant wildlife, medicinal plants and cultural presentations. Various other attractions are the giant *ceibo* tree, several salt licks and a sleeping roost of tropical birds. All of these are accessible by canoe on the Río Conambo.

The situation of Llanchamacocha and Jandiayacu is of particular interest, considering that ecotourism has been chosen as the only viable economic alternative to the Záparo's traditional subsistence-based lifestyle. The Záparos are seriously concerned with the impending threat of losing both their culture through assimilation into the surrounding Quichua populations, and their native environment, through the intrusive influence of oil companies. Now that CBE has been implemented, a reliable source of income will likely help empower the Záparo people to more fully embrace their rights and traditional heritage. Their strong social consciousness is demonstrated by the efficient running of their ecotourism project, characterized by an equal distribution of revenues within the community and their astute environmental sensitivity.

Visits to these communities typically last from three to five days; however, programs are flexible. Part of each program is spent in the communities, combined with a two-day descent by dugout canoe on the Río Conambo. The native guide, Ricardo Ushigua, is extremely helpful and encourages combination visits as long as they are geographically and temporally possible. If you really wish to enjoy and observe everything that Llanchamacocha and Jandiayacu have to offer, it would be wise to choose the longer program and perhaps even extend your trip by a few days.

Contact ATACAPI Tours one week in advance to make flight arrangements. The short 30-minute plane ride offers a spectacular view of the dense tropical landscape below. Prepare yourself for an interesting ride that ends on a short grass airstrip at the very heart of Llanchamacocha and a return flight from the new airstrip of Jandiayacu!

Price: $26 to $45/person/day (depending on group size) and $500 for the charter of a five-seater plane.

CURARAY (ATACAPI Tours)

Tourists with the financial capacity to charter a plane for the 35-minute flight from Shell to the Quichua community of Curaray will see a settlement rarely visited by outsiders, which offers an authentic first-hand experience of indigenous life on the Río Curaray. Emphasis is placed on a motorized canoe trip down-river to a series of strangely shaped, wildlife-rich oxbow lakes, with overnight stays in basic shelters. Fishing and birding enthusiasts will find a nirvana of sorts in this area. When the motor is turned off, the fishing lines and binoculars come out and you are slowly poled downriver by your guides.

Curaray is a grouping of five small communities with San José de Curaray, the main center, forming the social core. All are located near the confluence of the Río Villano with the Río Curaray. The communities are connected by foot trails including an impressive suspension bridge over the Río Curaray. Despite these trails, the rivers and the local airstrip are the main arteries, allowing people and goods to move in and out of the area. Your arrival by plane is sure to be greeted by excited community members and seen as an important inflow of information and goods.

As an association, the communities that comprise Curaray hold title to a 42 000 hectare territory known as block 16. Pavacachi's block 18 forms the eastern boundary while the Río Curaray itself serves as the northern border with Huaorani territory and Yasuní National Park. Inaccessible by road, Curaray's isolation is its strongest attraction, ensuring access to communally-owned intact primary rainforest and flooded forests.

The present *cabaña* complex has a capacity of six people, but has not been used since its construction in 1996 due to a lack of tourists. The location is ideal, only 20 minutes from the Jesús Cocha Lagoons. A dining room and non-functioning bathrooms (as of May, 1998) round out the main infrastructure. Planned lodging at this site is for one night only; other nights are spent camping on beaches in temporary shelters or with a local family. These are primitive accommodations catering to hardy travelers, with bathrooms rarely being more than the closest tree or bush while showers are nothing more than a dip in the chocolate colored waters of the Río Curaray.

Curaray presently offers both four and five-day programs. On the day of arrival, groups will be taken by their guide to a local family home where they spend their first night. Downriver travel to the lagoons begins on the second day with piranha fishing and jungle hikes as the main activities. Monkeys and birds are the most common forms of animal life observed during the day; caimans and alligators are the highlights of the evening. The five-day program includes a visit to the impressive Laguna Hursa Yacu, a large oxbow lake with an island in the center. The return trip upriver begins on the third day. Depending on the length of your program, you will reach the community either that night or the following afternoon. The final night will usually be spent at the *cabañas* or in a family home. A closing cultural presentation with drumming, dancing and a visit from the local *shaman* completes the tour on a festive note.

During the trip, the guides and assistants will set up camp and cook meals consisting of fresh fish and other local produce such as *yuca* and *plátanos*. *Chicha*, the local beverage of choice, will always be available. Keep in mind that the water used in its preparation and the water served to you may be unsafe to drink. A water purifier is a handy tool to prevent illness. Be sure to bring along enough staple foods to feed your group plus two extra persons (see Chapter XI, "Tips for Travelers").

Curaray's ecotourism project is a community owned enterprise designed to operate on a rotational system allowing equal participation by each family. An entrance fee is paid to the Associacíon de Curaray to be distributed equally between member communities and invested into communal funds. A joint venture with ATACAPI Tours since 1996 is designed to bring tourists into the area and to coordinate their arrival from Puyo.

Delfin Vargas, Curaray's ecotourism coordinator, is anxious to have small groups visit his community on a more regular basis. This enthusiasm is reflected in the effort that has been invested in the program over the past two years, despite the lack of visitors. This eagerness, combined with Curaray's cultural and natural richness, make it an ideal destination for travelers seeking isolation in a setting that has remained almost untouched by tourism.

Flying in the Oriente is always an adventure, half of which is just getting ready to leave! For your own security it is important that your preparations are done precisely and double checked for accuracy. First, weight constraints on the flight in will limit the amount of gear you can take with you. Fortunately, the community has mosquito nets and mattresses for its guests so weight can be saved for other things like gasoline. As a minimum, a five-day program for three persons (one canoe) requires 50 gallons of fuel whereas 30 gallons are required for four days. Motor oil in a ratio of 1 liter to 10 gallons of gas must be purchased as well. Failure to bring sufficient fuel will substantially restrict the quality of your visit and can lead to problems. In the case of an emergency, gasoline may be available in very limited quantities in San José de Curaray but at exorbitant prices and only after extensive, drunken negotiations.

Contact ATACAPI Tours a week in advance to make flight reservations and for help in coordinating fuel purchases. Present capacity of the Curaray program is from one to six people, with three being the preferred number. One motorized canoe and driver are required per three person group. The community also welcomes spontaneous arrivals of tourists who arrange the logistics (flight, food, fuel) on their own.

Price: The following prices apply to independent travelers making their own arrangements. ATACAPI Tours had not finalized its program plans, prices and arrangements with the Curaray community at the time of writing.

Entrance fee - $30/group, guide - $16/day/group (up to 6), canoe/motorist - 20$/day/3 persons, assistant motorist - $6/day, cook - $10/day/group, accomodations - $2/person/night, plus charter flight and extra gas for canoe trips.

Contact: ATACAPI Tours

CANELOS

Canelos is one of the longest-standing Quichua communities in the Pastaza area. Although ecotourism is still in its developmental stages, tourists seeking a relaxed and flexible setting will find that Canelos is easily accessible and has a lot to offer. Activities include moderate hiking, waterfall visits, canoe trips and the presentation of fine indigenous handicrafts.

There are 24 small communities within the territorial boundaries of Canelos. The Río Bobonaza, which runs through the center, traverses a landscape of rolling hills. Currently tourists are lodged at the Hotel Guatusaloca, comfortable and centrally located atop the hill in the main village of Canelos. The hotel can accommodate up to 23 people in 15 clean and secure rooms with electricity. There is a communal washroom with a shower and toilets. The running water is NOT safe to drink; however, the hotel plans to have potable well water in the near future. The building is presently under construction with the addition of four double rooms with private baths. The hotel restaurant serves three good meals a day and will accommodate vegetarians if you supply your own beans or other protein supplement, but expect slow service. There is also a general store and a dance bar (*discoteca*) on the ground level.

Tourists need only to bring personal belongings, rubber boots and a rain poncho when staying at the hotel; sandals and running shoes can be worn within the community. If you have an interest in camping or canoe trips, all food and sleeping gear (including a mosquito net) must be brought along.

A communally-owned *cabaña* complex lies an hour's walk down a winding, century-old cobblestone path and across the Río

Bobonaza. Lack of funding has prevented the installation of water, thus the project remains incomplete despite the fact that the *cabañas* are in good condition.

The tourism program offers many jungle walks including one to a beautiful 15–meter waterfall where one can swim and fish for catfish (*carrachama*). Wildlife is scarce near the settlements but a three–hour hike into the nearby jungle brings you to a zone of abundant wildlife where monkeys, *guantas*, boars and reptiles can be observed. You may combine any of the hikes with cultural activities such as those led by the women's cooperative, or by simply hanging out with the locals.

Canelos' ecotourism project involves 200 of the 800 community members under the organization of FENAQUIPA, a small group of Quichua around Canelos which separated from OPIP. The program is still young and lacks promotional links, but the small number of tourists who have been to Canelos have enjoyed their stay. Several qualified local guides work on a rotational basis and most either own or have access to a dugout paddle canoe. All tourist dollars spent in Canelos directly benefit the employees, artisans and community.

To get to Canelos, take a taxi or a bus for one and a half hours south from Puyo. Your best bet for an initial contact is through Ramon Garcés who is presently the Canelos Ecotourism Coordinator. He will be able to direct you to the available guides and help you to establish a program for the duration of your stay. The community is in the process of setting up contact numbers (either by radio or by phone) which should be available in Puyo by September of 1998, and at the hotel in Canelos by December.

The community prefers a group size of four to seven people; prices may be negotiated for groups of five or more.

Price: $15 to $25/person/day (depending on group size, 3days/2nights program).

Transportation to and from the community is not included; prices vary if overnights are spent in the jungle.

Contact: Ramon Garcés – Coordenador de Ecoturismo, FENAQUIPA, Casilla Postal #16-01-691, Puyo, Pastaza

PAVACACHI

A one-hour plane ride east from Shell over the dense tropical forest, lands you in a remote haven bordering on Yasuní National Park, where a diversity of flora and fauna abound. This Quichua venture is attractive to the nature lover who is willing to pay for comfortable accommodations and good service in a distinctive setting. Tourists can choose between a "hard" program, geared towards those with higher physical capabilities and a more profound interest in the surrounding ecology, and a "soft", less strenuous program that makes for a pleasant overview of the area.

The Forest Association of "Beautiful Valley" (ASOFVH) is a small community located on the Río Curaray just inside the Yasuní Park boundary. The tourism program, centered 15 minutes downriver by motorized canoe from the settlement, is run by a group of ASOFH community members who have formed the private enterprise of Acangau Ruta Verde Tour (ARVETUR). Pavacachi's tourism complex, Ñucanchi Huasi, is comprised of two fully equipped sleeping *cabañas* with capacity for 10 people, a cooking/eating hut, a sheltered meeting/hammock room, and a bathroom boasting two toilets and showers with running water. Accommodations are rustic but quite comfortable. The food is a delicious mix of indigenous and national products prepared over an open fire. Vegetarians are readily accommodated, but beware: they don't consider their staple Maggi chicken broth to be a meat product!

Pavacachi offers five principal services: jungle guiding through primary forest, river transport by dugout paddle or motor canoe, meal service, sleeping accommodations, and a traditional cultural program in the community center. Typical programs last anywhere from four to 15 days. Natural attractions include the Río Curaray where one can fish and swim, several oxbow lakes, isolated lagoons, and an immense expanse of primary jungle. Loosely defined foot trails allow guests an intimate jungle experience. You will invariably encounter a wide variety of exquisite insects, numerous medicinal plants, and if you are lucky, a glimpse of some of the surrounding fauna. Pavacachi's remote location provides a good chance to see native wildlife in action, especially on dry, sunny days when animals gather at the natural salt licks. The Spanish-speaking guides are very competent, providing the tourist with an enlightened view of their natural environment.

Jungle exploration programs away from the central *cabañas* can be extended over several days. Personnel offer overnight camping under rudimentary, yet functional plastic tarps on any one of the sandy beaches bordering the Río Curaray. In planning for this activity, tourists should bring an air mattress, a sleeping bag or sheet, a mosquito net and plenty of insect repellent. Pavacachi provides lifejackets and has several pairs of rubber boots in large sizes; to ensure a proper fit, it is best to bring your own. Future plans for the project include more beds at the existing Ñucanchi Huasi *cabañas* as well as the construction of new *cabañas* at another jungle location.

Pavacachi played a key role as one of the four founding members in the formation of ATACAPI Tours in 1994 (see "ATACAPI Tours"). Internal problems in 1996 prompted members of the ASOFVH to initiate the Acangau Tours enterprise for more autonomous control and further development of their community tourism program. Profits are divided between administrative costs of the operation and the members directly involved in the ecotourism venture. They are extremely well organized and are in the process of developing new programs, possibly including one to Curaray in the near future. At present four CETUR-certified guides are employed by Acangau Tour. All speak good Spanish, but none are fluent in English; you may want to bring a translator guide with you.

Access to this remote location is solely by light aircraft (five or 12 passengers). A spectacular one-hour flight over pristine primary forest from the Shell airport (a 15-minute drive from Puyo) lands you at the Pavacachi airstrip. A 15-minute canoe ride down the Río Curaray brings you to the Ñucanchi Huasi *cabaña* complex. A military permit must be sought in Shell prior to departure - bring a color, passport-size photo. Arrangements should be made as far in advance as possible; however, Acangau Tours is fairly flexible and last-minute requests are generally accommodated.

Prices: $92/person/day (includes air transport, food, guiding etc.)
Contact: Acangau Ruta Verde Cia. Lta. (ARVETUR) - Raúl Tapuy V., Calle Río Amazonas, Shell, Pastaza, telefax: (09) 353 883 Tropic Ecological Adventures. Tel. (593 2) 225 907, 234 594, fax (593 2) 560 756, e-mail: tropic@uio.satnet.net, www.tropiceco.com

KAPAWI

Located in the remotest part of the Ecuadorian Amazon Basin, the Kapawi Ecological Reserve represents a novel sustainable development project implemented by the private tour operator, CANODROS S.A., in partnership with the Federation of Ecuadorian Achuar Nationalities (FINAE). Its luxury eco-lodge is majestically nestled on the edge of a small lagoon surrounded entirely by primary rainforest. This isolated area is pristine habitat for many jungle species, providing an ideal observatory for affluent bird and animal watchers. In short, Kapawi provides high-class ecotourism in a jungle setting, thoroughly enhanced by authentic indigenous influence.

The hotel complex is located just off the Río Pastaza only a short distance before it reaches the Peruvian border. It includes 20 waterfront cabañas with capacity for 40 guests, two central buildings with bar, lounge, kitchen and dining room facilities, and a separate hammock room with a central fire pit. The infrastructure was built in typical Achuar style with local jungle products; not a single metal nail was used in the entire construction! One hundred and fifty local Achuar were hired to build the complex over a two year period; it opened for business in April of 1996.

CANODROS S.A. has invested heavily in making the operation as ecologically friendly as possible. It has installed a photovoltaic system which provides 85 percent of the required electrical current. Solar heated water provides hot showers (rationed to five gallons per person per day) for which biodegradable soap is furnished. Raised boardwalks connect all the cabañas, greatly reducing erosion. A septic system manages human waste, and non-biodegradable garbage is separated for maximum recycling and flown out by plane for disposal. When possible, electric canoe motors are used to reduce noise and pollution. In addition, the entire complex has been built on the edge of the lagoon, partially over the water, to avoid destruction of the surrounding forest.

Typically, tourist programs run with less than 10 people per group. Activities are led by one of three Spanish-speaking Achuar guides and a biologist who acts as a co-guide and Spanish-English translator. Tours offer a mix of exposure to both the cultural and natural attractions of the area.

The lodge itself lies a half–hour canoe ride away from Kapawi Center, the largest of the six surrounding communities which can be visited for a personal experience of Achuar culture. A typical visit includes stopping at a local house to sit with the family, talk and drink *chicha*. When offered a bowl of the traditional indigenous drink, courtesy requires that you should at least pretend to sip from the bowl; however, be aware that the water used to make it may not be purified (ask your guide to be sure). Some villages may have handicrafts for sale, but if not, the lodge boutique stocks locally made items. Other cultural attractions in the area include typical meals either in a community or at the hotel, learning about and participating in shamanic rituals, and a demonstration of the technique of blowgun hunting where tourists are invited to join in.

The natural landscape in the area is exquisite. The reserve is an excellent location for birdwatching with over 520 species identified so far. There are also possibilities of seeing caimans, freshwater dolphins, monkeys, peccaries, anacondas, and if you are extremely lucky, a jaguar, among others. An extensive network of walking and hiking trails has been developed to serve a range of physical capabilities. These can be combined with canoe rides (either motor or dugout paddle), and for the more ambitious and athletically adept, multi-day camping trips can be organized. The jungle foot trails and series of interconnected rivers and lagoons provide a varied landscape to explore and discover.

The atmosphere at Kapawi is friendly and tranquil, and guests will feel that their every need is catered to. There's no need to worry about food; the mix of national and international cuisine is varied and delicious. As there are no fixed programs, you can decide with your guide which itinerary suits you best. Of course there is always the option of lazing in your hammock with a mixed drink in your hand!

CANODROS S.A. is, for the moment, operating the hotel and pays $2 000 per month to FINAE for rental and usage rights of the area. The money is divided between the five community associations which make up FINAE, including the community of Kapawi which owns the land on which the hotel is built. As well, FINAE receives $10 per tourist entering into the area (not included in the package price). The majority of the employees in the hotel are Achuar, and as the idea is to give full management of the operation to the Associación Amunti (of the five communities surrounding Kapawi) in the year 2011, CANODROS S.A. is working to provide the indigenous employees with adequate management and language skills. So far the project seems to reflect a positive relationship between the company and the local Achuars.

Over the past year 520 guests have visited Kapawi, some through direct contact with CANODROS S.A. and others through organizations such as Tropic Ecological Adventures, Wilderness Travel, Adventure Travel, The Nature Conservancy, Pacha Mama, Galapagos Inc., Archipel, Aequator, Field Guides, Victor Emanuel, and Kleintours, each of which may offer Kapawi as part of a package deal. There is much scope for both group and individual activities for any age and ability level, as well as relaxation and leisure time during your stay. Visits can be anywhere from four to eight days.

With the nearest road a 12–day day hike away, access to the area is only possible by small aircraft. Tourist flights leave from Quito, Shell, Baños, Cuenca or Macas and touch down in either Sharamentsa or Wayusentsa. From there, a one and a half hour ride by covered motor canoe takes you to the hotel dock. Kapawi provides visitors with rubber boots, rain ponchos, umbrellas, water bottles, lifejackets, towels and soap, so pack lightly, as baggage capacity on the aircraft is limited. Be sure to make arrangements in advance.

Price: $75 to $100/person/day (depending on the length of stay, based on double occupancy) plus the $250 flight.

Contact: CANODROS S.A., Luis Urdaneta 1418 y Av. del Ejército, PO Box 09-01-8442, Guayaquil, tel.: (593 4) 285 711, 280 173, 280 143, fax: (593 4) 287 651, e-mail:ecotourism@canodros.com.ec, http://www.canodros.com

CANODROS S.A., Air Center No. 1138, PO Box 52-2970, Miami, FL 33152, USA

XI
TIPS FOR TRAVELERS

TRAVEL ADVICE

You've read the books, picked your communities and are ready to go. . . . What's next? Regardless of your experience, all travelers can use a checklist and a bit of advice to help them on their way. The authoring team collaborated to reflect on their needs, desires and experiences in the Oriente, and believe that the following will be helpful to pack you up and send you off prepared, so that you will return with one of the greatest experiences of your life!

For the benefit of both tourists and community members, a few "do's" and "don'ts" are recommended:

~ Be open to different appreciations of what is normal. For example, punctuality is not an Amazon concept.

~ Don't take someone's photo unless you've asked their permission first. Don't be offended if they refuse.

~ Don't be ostentatious with wealth and material posessions.

~ Hang on to any trash you generate like plastics, dead batteries etc. until you get back to the nearest urban center.

~ Always wear insect repellent, even in the tight spots under your clothes.

~ Wear a strong sunblock and a hat or cap when it is sunny.

~ Wear a rain poncho or similar when it rains.

~ Avoid putting your hand where you can't see it, or leaning on a tree trunk without first looking. There may be thorns, biting ants (the 2 cm long conga is quite painful), or prickly caterpillars.

~   Always carry your passport and money with you.

~   Be aware of dirty or diseased animals (especially dogs); don't pet them!

~   Waterproof all your belongings (humidity and moisture are inevitable, and it has been proven that things never dry in the jungle).

~   Ask before doing any non-program activities (ex. don't take off with the community canoe!).

~   Indigenous people tend to shake hands often and quite gently (like a hand pat), so be careful not to shake their arms off!

~   *"Buenos días", "por favor", "gracias"* is always appreciated.

~   Communities engage in numerous fiestas and special events, many of which are scheduled on short notice (Saint's day, *mingas*, soccer tournaments); others are well anticipated (Mother's and Father's Month!). This may unexpectedly interfere with your program but is an opportunity for intercultural exchange.

Keep in mind that international communication from the jungle is a lengthy process. It's not that your hearing is delayed - telephones are badly connected. Mail service is available but is much slower. In addition, the rare banks in jungle towns do not always open or change money at convenient hours. Some may close very early in the day and many will not change money after 1pm, so don't leave your money changing to the last minute! It is also important to ensure that all bills are tear-free because banks are picky - don't argue, just take care of your *dinero*!

FOOD

As a basic part of our lives, the concept of food is straight forward. However, since you are about to enter a different world, you may need some advice. The majority of the ecotourism projects will provide the necessary provisions although some of the more remote or newly developed ecotourism programs will request that tourists bring their own food supply with them for the duration of their program.

All indigenous communities produce staple foods such as bananas, *plátanos*, *yuca* and papayas and in most communities, an indigenous cook will prepare a combination of traditional indigenous and Ecuadorian foods. If you are taking food supplies, bring a little extra in case you end up feeding more than just your group (community members will love you for it!). Ideal foods to bring are non-perishable and canned goods, but not too many of the latter because they tend to be bulky and heavy (taking some of your favourites is a great opportunity for an intercultural exchange). If you want to bring gifts for your community, think educational and useful. Avoid the temptation to give cigarettes; they are addictive and can create new and unnecessary demands on very low incomes. If you are vegetarian, brace yourself. The concept of conscientiously preparing a meatless meal is new to many of the communities, so don't be surprised if your request for vegetarian food produces a plate of rice, beans and lettuce. Bringing high protein foods or multivitamins is a good idea.

You will see many animals in the forest and, depending on your community, you may also see them on your plate. Do not be offended by this - it is an integral part of many indigenous diets. However, do not encourage your guide to bring such rarities home for you - catching such prey is hard work and hunting to satisfy curious tourists will degrade indigenous food supplies. In such a situation the tourist should not wear hungry eyes - the indigenous people are very humble and many will sacrifice their needs for the tourist. If, however, you are offered some wild game, try to refuse it graciously so as not to offend their generosity.

It is nearly impossible to visit an indigenous community without savoring the typical indigenous drink called "*chicha*". This beverage is typically made from chewed *yuca* or other starchy crops and is prepared only by the indigenous women. When left to ferment over time, *chicha* becomes a potent alcoholic mixture which may not always agree with your taste buds. Try to control your facial expression and just say "yucka" - this will be perceived as ingredient identification rather than expression of disgust. If you're lucky you will get it while it's fresh - the *indígenas* swear that three bowls in the morning provide enough fuel to work all day! Overall, just remember to keep an open mind when sampling traditional foods. They may be very different and strange but they will definitely be the cultural aspect of your trip which you will never forget.

CLEANLINESS, FIRST AID,
AND AILMENTS IN THE JUNGLE

It is important to remember that once you are in a community, a Western doctor may be a long hike or drive away. Start off healthy and be prepared. The following are items to bring and advice that one should consider.

The jungle is full of weird and wonderful things - for everything that could harm you on your journey (including traveler's tummy!) there is usually a medicinal plant remedy in the jungle, in addition to the possibility of helpful *shaman* knowledge. These are options that should not be overlooked - many natives depend on them for their survival. However, your body may not be used to such treatments, so abnormalities and serious health concerns should be given professional attention immediately.

Vaccines: Your doctor will recommend numerous vaccinations for tropical travel - the most important in the Oriente are yellow fever and anti-malarial pills. Both must be in your system seven to 10 days before jungle exposure, depending on the prescription. If these are not received before leaving home, they may be obtained in major urban centers in Ecuador. There is a tropical medicine clinic in Quito which is clean, inexpensive and gives stamped "yellow cards". It is easy to get an appointment: phone Dr. Rosenberg (233-333) or stop by the clinic at Mariscal Foch 467 y Almagro. The International Association for Medical Assistance to Travelers (IAMAT) is another option - for more information or membership application contact http://www.sentex.net/~iamat or iamat@sentex.net.

Personal Stink: Be responsible and efficient; bring multi-purpose, biodegradable cleaning products. Pure Liquid Castille (mint) Soap has been recommended - use it to clean your whole self (including your teeth!) and clothes too. The best anti-perspirant/deodorant in the hot, wet jungle is some form of talc and/or baby powder; cornstarch and/or baking soda serve the same purpose and are unscented. Generally try to avoid scented products; however, citronella, lemon/lime juice, cedar, lavender, and cloves are known to offend the bugs. Baby wipes are handy - they could be the equivalent of your shower.

For the *Chicas*: Menstruation is a fact of life, so plan ahead. Bring enough supplies for the duration of your travels and remember - you have to carry your garbage out with you! An enviro-friendly and convenient solution to consider is the "KEEPER" - a reusable rubber cup that is worn internally. Look in health and enviro shops or contact the company at 1-800-680-9739, http://www.magi.com/~keeper, or keeper@magi.com.

Prescriptions: Whether it's personal medicine or eyewear, bring your prescriptions with you! Contact lens wearers might want to bring a small mirror and may consider daily wear lenses for sanitary purposes - but pack any wastes out with you!

~   First Aid:
      Tiger Balm - a multi-purpose life saver for sore muscles, decongestion and relieving bug bites!
~   insect Repellent - there are many brands but nothing beats DEET, though *Avon Skin So Soft* oil is the best for sand flies
~   sunscreen (generally more expensive when bought in Ecuador)

~   Tylenol / Ibuprofen - they kill pain, reduce fevers, and are
    nice on already sensitive foreign stomachs
~   anti-diarrhea pills - so that you, rather than your bowels,
    can be on the move
~   rehydration packets - in case the above does not work
~   mole or second skin (for blisters), iodine or alcohol pads,
    band-aids and/or gauze and waterproof tape (duct tape can
    be a substitute)
~   antifungal foot powder for wet feet
~   water purification pump or pills (a pump offers best pro-
    tection and is a good investment; it should purify and filter
    viruses, bacteria and protozoa (especially giardia); a cou-
    ple of drops of pure bleach will purify a liter of water)
~   Solarcaine lotion - another multi-purpose product for
    burns, bites, and preventing chiggers!
~   throat lozenges and familiar cold medicines
~   scissors, tweezers, and/or a multi-purpose knife

Good Reference Books: <u>Wilderness and Travel Medicine</u>, by Eric
A. Weiss, MD; <u>Where there is no Doctor</u>, by David Werner.

Possible Encounters: This is a list of medical situations that some
of our group members encountered on their travels; these are possibilities but not everyday occurrences, so don't panic when reading this.
~   chiggers - ticks that form prominent bumps on your skin
    and itch like mad! Beware of short grass (where they thrive)
    and tight clothing (where they like to be - nice warm spots)
~   colds - from being wet, and temperature changes
~   animal bites - even the cute furry ones bite! (stitches and
    rabies shots may be needed)

~ amoebas - from water and fresh veggies - they will swim in your stomach and make toilet runs an hourly activity

~ some form of bot fly maggot/possible flesh eating bacteria. Anti-biotics are often prescribed (so know your allergies). There is a medication to clean your system of amoebas - but it is only available in the city, so be careful!

BE WISE… The best medicine is prevention

~ do not aggravate bites, cuts, and other skin irritations

~ bathing in the river does not guarantee you're clean - even if you use soap!

~ swim and bathe appropriately - do not pee in the water! This can attract aquatic creatures that could lead to serious complications, and contaminate bathing and drinking water downstream.

CLOTHING

Clothes should be a major consideration when planning to visit the Oriente. You must adopt a practical mentality. To reduce your luggage when visiting the more remote regions, choose only lightweight clothing and pack only the essentials. The monkeys aren't concerned about how you look (or how you smell, for that matter) so leave your city clothes in storage (hostels, South American Explorers Club) in Quito before entering the Amazon - otherwise you'll come back with mouldy jeans! Above all, water-proof all your clothing and equipment to prevent moisture from entering (good ol' ziplocks!). Quick-dry fibres/materials are also ideal for preventing the degradation of clothes in the hot and humid environment. Dark colors are an excellent way of hiding the dirt and being less visible to the jungle wildlife. Light colors, however, are ideal for distracting those crazy buzzing insects, so intermediate colors are your best choice. Since dirt will not be too visible on them, you can get away with packing only a few changes of clothes! All major towns in the Oriente have laundry facilities which take up to two days or, if you're lucky, only a few hours. To make packing a little less confusing, refer to the follow-ing:

~   pants that zip-off into shorts (no canvas!)
~   at least 2 T-shirts (preferably old and ugly ones)
~   1 long-sleeved shirt or sweatshirt (no big sweaters)
~   rain gear or solid poncho
~   bathing suit and fast-drying towel
~   rubber boots with treads - fancy hiking boots are not for the
     jungle. Rubber boots can be bought in any major jungle

town but the biggest size is 10, so bigfoots should buy them at home. Inserting soles will make rubber boots more comfortable (make sure to test-walk them). If you're not crazy about the rubber idea you may want to bring along some jungle boots for more comfort, stability and traction.

~ 2 pairs of quick-dry socks (or just wear the same pair of wet ones until they become mouldy)

~ light running shoes, sandals or thongs (flip-flop sandals, not fancy underwear!)

~ hat or bandana (indispensable!)

EQUIPMENT

There is no doubt that traveling in the jungle requires a number of items which will determine the success of your journey. Jungle tours are fraught with unpredictability, so keep in mind that your equipment is your survival kit against the elements. Maps are not essential but can be useful for some of the tours. When applicable 1: 50 000 IGM sheet I.D. numbers are provided in the community descriptions. These maps are available from the Instituto Geográfico Militar (IGM) in Quito.

The following items are what all jungle travelers must bring:

~   Swiss army knife
~   1 liter water bottle or water pouch
~   candle or flashlight to get around in the obscurity of the jungle night; extra batteries
~   sleeping mat or light thermarest- if you go to a community that does not provide one
~   light sleeping bag or sheet- again, if necessary.
~   mosquito net, if not provided.
~   camera with mix of 50 ASA and 400 ASA film because of contrasting light availability on rivers and in the forest.
~   binoculars for bird and animal watching
~   toilet paper (this is as important as your passport - keep it on hand at all times!)
~   a day pack of sturdy material
~   a good book to read (for those endless river boat rides!), journal and Spanish dictionary
~   water resistant watch or travel alarm clock
~   sunglasses

~ ear plugs (for loud, early morning roosters!)
~ rope or cord for clotheslines and mosquito nets- if necessary.
~ plastic bags of different sizes (ziplocks are great!)
~ duct tape (you will be amazed at how multi-functional this can be)
~ waterproof matches; sewing or repair kit
~ first-aid kit
~ passport, health card, and health insurance (and photocopies - not all in one place!)
~ pictures of your country and family for intercultural exchange
~ and finally, a big backpack (to carry it all!)

Army surplus and outdoor shops are wonderlands for your pre-jungle preparations. Being prepared before you leave means that the only thing left to do is have fun!

ENJOY YOUR RESPONSIBLE ADVENTURES!

GLOSSARY

AACLLAC	— Asociación Antonio Cerda de Llaucana Cocha
agroforestry	— interplanting of trees with crops and pasture
aquaculture	— fish cultivation (in ponds in the case of the Oriente)
artesanía	— handicrafts made locally by community members
ARVETUR	— Acangau Ruta Verde Tour
ASOFVH	— Forest Association of "Beautiful Valley"
balsa wood	— a tropical tree with a lightweight wood, often used to build rafts
boardwalk	— elevated walk-way covered with sawn boards
cabaña	— building constructed from local material for ecotourism purposes
caiman	— a South American reptile resembling an alligator
caminata	— a walk through the jungle
capivara	— the world's largest rodent, typical of swampy areas
CBE	— community based ecotourism
cernidora	— a flour and rice sifter made from palm fiber
ceibo	— Spanish spelling of ceiba tree
centro	— a center
CETUR	— Ecuadorian Tourism Corporation
chacra	— a small-scale clearing used for subsistence agriculture by indigenous people
chicha	— a typical indigenous beverage made from yuca or other starchy crops which becomes alcoholic when left to ferment
cinchona tree	— a tree which yields the anti-malarial ingredient quinine

cloud forest	— forest at 2500-3400 m elevation drenched by upwelling air masses
COICA	— Coordinating Body of Indigenous Peoples of the Amazon Basin
colonos	— colonists or settlers from highland or coastal Ecuador
comedor	— kitchen/dining room, commons
CONAIE	— Confederation of Indigenous Nationalities of Ecuador
CONFENIAE	— Confederation of Indigenous Nationalities of the Ecuadorian Amazon
DED	— Deutscher Entwicklungsdienst (German Development Service)
despedida	— a farewell ceremony
discoteca	— a dance platform where drinks may be sold
ethnobiology	— the study of indigenous use of plants
FCUNAE	— Federation of Communes and Native Union of the Ecuadorian Amazon (in fact the Quichua federation of the middle and lower Napo)
FENAQUIPA	— Federation of Quichua Nationalities of Pastaza (in fact a small grouping in the Canelos area)
fauna	— animals of a specific area
fiesta	— a celebration or festivity
FINAE	— Interprovincial Federation of Ecuadorian Achuar Nationalities
flora	— plants of a specific area
FOIN	— Federation of Indigenous Organizations of Napo, the Quichua federation of the Upper Napo
guanta	— a large rodent trapped by indigenous people for food

horticulture	— gardening; intensive small-scale agriculture
Hoatzin	— a rather noisy, prehistoric looking bird found in flocks on lake margins
indígena	— an indigenous person
INEFAN	— The Ecuadorian Institute of Forestry, Natural Areas and Wildlife
intercambio cultural	— intercultural exchange
intercropping	— a mixture of various crops
jaguarundi	— a species in the family of the wild cat
laguna	— lagoon
latrine	— an outdoor toilet sheltered in a hut
macho bravado	— male swagger displayed by some non-indigenous guides
minga	— a community work party
mirador	— a look-out with panoramic view
motorista	— a motor canoe driver
multiethnic	— having a number of ethnicities
NGO	— non-governmental organization
OINCE	— Organization of the Cofan Indigenous Nationality of Ecuador
OISE	— Siecoya Indigenous Organization of Ecuador
ONHAE	— Organization of the Huaorani Nationality of the Ecuadorian Amazon
ONISE	— Organization of the Siona Indigenous Nationality of Ecuador
OPIP	— Organization of Indigenous Peoples of Pastaza
Oriente	— the Ecuadorian Amazon
oxbow lake	— former river meander, cut off when the river broke through the narrow neck of the meander

páramo — humid high-altitude grassland of South America between 3 400 and 4 500 m elevation

patron-peon relationship — dependency relation between traditional employer and rural laborer

pirana — extremely voracious South American fish

piscicultura — fish raising or fish farm

plátano — plantain

puente — a bridge

puerto — a port

quilla — a small dugout canoe without a motor, which is paddled or poled

ranchera — open-sided "bus" used on local routes in the tropical lowlands

RICANCIE — Network of Indigenous Communities of the Upper Napo for Intercultural Exchange and Ecotourism

río — river

saladero — a salt lick

selva — jungle

selva alta — upper jungle, above 600 m elevation

selva baja — lowland jungle, below 600 m elevation

serbatana — blowgun used for hunting purposes

shaman — spiritual leader and traditional medicinal doctor of a community

shigra — handbag

siesta — an afternoon nap

socio — a community member

speleology — the exploration and discovery of caves

tarabita — a cable with platform suspended on rollers, used to cross rivers

thatched roof

cabaña — *cabaña* with roof made of palm leaves

vía — a route or road

yagé — hallucinogenic plant

yuca — a starchy tuber crop of the tropics

ANNOTATED BIBLIOGRAPHY

Asociación Ecuatoriana de Ecoturismo (ASEC)
1998   *Políticas y Estratégias para la Participación Comunitaria en el Ecoturismo.* Quito: ASEC.

Balik, M.J., Elisabetsky, E. and Laird, S.A.
1996   *Medicinal Resources of the Tropical Forest.* New York: Columbia University Press. Comprehensive source of information on tropical plants and their medicinal use with a section on conservation efforts and economic benefits for indigenous people.

Bebbington, A. et al.
1992   *Autores de una Década Ganada: Tribus, Comunidades y Campesinos en la Modernidad.* Quito: COMUNIDEC. Description of the increasingly effective social and political organization of indigenous peoples during the 1980s, with a section on the Amazon.
       ABY

Box, B., ed.
1997   *South American Handbook.* Bath: Footprint Handbooks, 74th edition.

BMZ
1995   *Ecotourism as a Conservation Instrument? Making Conservation Projects more Attractive.* pp. 243-297. Federal Ministry for Economic Cooperation and Development, Research Report no. 177. Cologne: Weltforum Verlag. Section comprising a good overview of tourism in the Cuyabeno Wildlife Reserve.

Benitez, L. y Garces, A.
   1992   *Culturas Ecuatorianas: Ayer y Hoy.* Sexta Ed. Quito: Abya
          Yala. In-depth description of the different indigenous cultures
          and communities of the Ecuadorian Amazon. Includes a good
          overview of Amazonian indigenous languages.
          ABY and LM

Caliano, M. y Gonsalo, J.A.
   1995   *Los Ai del Río Aguarico, Mito y Cosmovisión.* Quito:
          Ediciones Abya-Yala. Mythology and cosmology of the Cofan.
          AA

Canaday, C. and Jost, L.
   1997   *Common Birds of Amazonian Ecuador.* Quito: Ediciones Libri
          Mundi. Complete and concise with vivid images. Highly rec-
          ommended.
          LM

Carlos, E., Céron, M. and Consuelo G. Montalvo.
   1998   *Ethnobotánica de los Huaorani de Quehueire Ono, Napo-
          Ecuador.* Quito: Ediciones Abya Yala.
          ABY

Ceballos-Lascuraín, H.
   1996   *Tourism, Ecotourism and Protected Areas.* Gland: IUCN.
          Study of the link between ecotourism and the conservation of
          protected areas with examples from all continents.

Cerda, C.
   1998   Personal communication with Cesar Cerda, President of OPIP.
Chiriboga, L. y Cruz, S.
   1992   *Retrato de la Amazonía.* Quito: Ediciones Libri Mundi.
          LM

COICA
   1989   Two Agendas on Amazon Development. *Cultural Survival Quarterly* 13 (4): 75-78. A manifesto demanding a leading role for indigenous peoples in the conservation of the Amazon rainforest.

COICA-CONFENIAE
   1993   *Ecoturismo: Lineamientos Basicos de una Propuesta Política para el Manejo del Ecoturismo en los Territorios de las Nacionalidades Indígenas de la Amazonía Ecuatoriana.* Unpublished manuscript, Quito.

Colby, G. and Dennet, C.
   1995   *Thy Will be Done: The Conquest of the Amazon; Nelson Rockefeller and Evangelism in the Age of Oil.*

Colvin, J.G.
   1994   Capirona: A Model of Indigenous Ecotourism. *Journal of Sustainable Tourism* 2 (3): 174-177. Informative and critical history of tourism in Capirona and its influence on community-based tourism within the Napo region.

Drumm, A.
   1991   *Integrated Impact Assessment of Nature Tourism in Ecuador's Amazon Region.*Quito: FEPROTUR.
           AT

Drumm, A.
   1993   *Ecotourism Versus the Oil Industry in the Cuyabeno Wildlife Reserve.* Paper presented at the Second World Congress on Tourism for the Environment, Margarita Island, September 27th-October 2nd, 1993.
           AT

1995   *Converting from Nature Tourism to Ecotourism in the Ecuadorian Amazon.* Paper presented at World Conference on Sustainable Tourism, Canary Islands, April 23rd-29th, 1995.
       AT

1997   *El Ecoturismo Como una Alternativa de Desarrollo Para los Pueblos Indígenas de la Amazonía.* Paper presented at the Seminario Regional de Ecoturismo, Comunidad de Capirona, November 23rd-28th, 1997.
       AT

1998   *New Approaches to Community-based Ecotourism Management* - Learning from Ecuador. In Ecotourism - A Guide for Planners and Managers, Volume 2, eds. Lindberg, K., Epler Wood, M., Engeldrum, D. pp. 197-214.
       TES

Emmons, L.
1990   *Neotropical Rainforest Mammals.* Chicago: University of Chicago Press. Guide to the mammals of South America's rainforest.
       LM

Epler Wood, M.
1998   *Meeting the Global Challenge of Community Participation in Ecotourism: Case Studies and Lessons from Ecuador.* Arlington, VA: The Nature Conservancy. NGO report on the problems and prospects of community based ecotourism with three cases from the Amazon.
       TES

Fundación Natura
   1992   *Acciones de Desarrollo y Areas Naturales Protegidas en el Ecuador. Reserva Faunística Cuyabeno.* Quito: Fundación Natura.

Fundación Natura
   1992   *Acciones de Desarrollo y Areas Naturales Protegidas en el Ecuador. Parque Nacional Yasuní y Reserva Biológica Limoncocha.* Quito: Fundación Natura.

Gentry, A.
   1996   *A Field Guide to the Families and Genera of Woody Plants of Northwest South America (Columbia, Ecuador, Peru).* Chicago: University of Chicago Press. Unique and easy to read guide on plants of northwestern South America.

Green, C.
   1996   *Birding Ecuador,* 2nd ed. Tucson, Arizona: Clive Green, 1208 North Swan Road. Recent guide leading you to spectacular bird spots in Ecuador.
          LM

INEFAN-GTZ.
   1996   Mapa del Nororiente del Ecuador: Situación Legal de las Tierras. Quito: IGM.

   1998   *Guía de Parques Nacionales y Reservas del Ecuador. Proyecto Protección de la Biodiversidad.* Quito: INEFAN/GEF.

Izko, X.
   1995   *Ecoturismo en el Ecuador: Trayectorias y Desafíos.* Quito: DDA, INTERCOOPERATION, IUCN. Ecotourism conference proceedings including case studies of Capirona and Zábalo.

Kane, J.

     1995   *Savages.* New-York: Alfred A. Knopf, Inc. Detailed and easy to read description of the Huaorani depicting their current problems and struggles.

          LM

Kimmerling, J.

     1990   *Amazon Crude.* Washington, D.C.: Natural Resources Defense Council. Analysis of the ecological and cultural impacts of petroleum development in the Ecuadorian Amazon with focus on the indigenous peoples.

          ABY

Labaca, M.A.

     1989   *Crónica Huaorani.* Pompeya: CICAME. Missionary perspective on the Huaorani.

Lemky, K.M.K.

     1992   *The Amazon Ecotourism Industry of Napo, Ecuador.* Unpublished M.A. thesis, Department of Geography, University of Ottawa. Description of the ecotourism industry with emphasis on the Napo region and impacts on the local economy of two types of tourists. Evaluation of prospects towards sustainable development.

Mabberley, D.J.

     1992   *Tropical Rain Forest Ecology.* Chapman and Hall. A detailed and highly technical source of information on the complexity of rainforest interactions.

Macdonald Jr., T.

     1981   Indigenous Response to an Expanding Frontier: Jungle Quichua Economic Conversion to Cattle Ranching. In *Cultural Transformations and Ethnicity in Modern Ecuador,*

ed. N.E. Whitten Jr., pp.356-383. Urbana: University of Illinois Press. Paper outlining the involuntary shift of the Pascu Urcu Runa on the Río Arajuno from shifting cultivation to cattle ranching. Valuable source of information on colonist influences.
ABY (Spanish version)

Mc Laren, D.

1998   *Rethinking Tourism and Ecotravel.* West Hartford: Kumarian Press. A good overview on the ethics of ecotourism.

Miller, C. and Halberstadt, J.

Ecuador Explorer, Definitive Guide to Ecuador. http:\\www.ecuadorexplorer.com, 1997. Very helpful resource for logistical aspects of traveling. The site provides the tourist with basic and detailed information on travel in Ecuador.

Ortiz de Villalba, J. S.

1984   *Los Ultimos Huaorani.* Pompeya: CICAME.
ABY

Paymal, N. and Sosa, C.

1993   *Amazon Worlds: Peoples and Cultures of Ecuador's Amazon Region.* Quito: Sinchi Sacha Foundation. Beautifully illustrated coffee table book on indigenous cultures of the Ecuadorian Amazon.
ABY and LM (Spanish version)

Rachowiecki, R. and Wagenhauser, B.

1997   *Climbing and Hiking in Ecuador,* 4th ed. Hunter Publishing. Best guide for hikers and mountain climbers, including several hikes in the Amazon.

1997   *Ecuador and the Galapagos Islands,* 4th ed. Hawthorn: Lonely Planet Publications. A popular guide for adventurous and low-budget travelers.
        LM

Redford, K.H. and Stearman, A.M.
    1993   Forest-Dwelling Native Amazonians and the Conservation of Biodiversity: Interests in Common or in Collision? *Conservation Biology 7 (2)*: 248-255. An article which questions whether *indígenas* are conservationists in the Western sense.

Rival, L.
    1996   *Hijos del Sol, Padres del Jaguar: Los Huaorani de Ayer y Hoy.* Quito: Abya Yala.
        ABY and LM
        Doctoral dissertation on changing Huaorani culture.

Schaller, D.T.
    1996   *Indigenous Ecotourism and Sustainable Development: The Case of Río Blanco, Ecuador.* Unpublished M.A. thesis, Department of Geography, University of Minnesota. Available at http://www.eduweb.com/schaller/. Detailed case study of Río Blanco, a Quichua community affiliated with RICANCIE which examines the benefits of ecotourism. Amazon Interactive: The Ecotourism Game, http://www.geog.umn.edu/~schaller/amazon/ecotourism/eco.html, 1996. Computer game based on the preceding study.

Smith, R.
    1993   *Crisis Under the Canopy: Tourism and Other Problems Facing the Present Day Huaorani.* Quito: Abya Yala. Bilingual (Spanish/English) book providing a comprehensive and

detailed description of the recent history and current problems faced by the Huaorani communities with particular focus on tourism.
ABY and LM (Spanish version)

1996 *Manual de Ecoturismo Para Guías y Comunidades Indígenas de la Amazonía Ecuatoriana.* Cayambe-Ecuador: Gráficas Modelo. Descriptive and technical book covering logistical aspects of guiding in the Ecuadorian Amazon.
ABY and LM

Terborgh, J.
1992 *Diversity and the Tropical Rain Forest.* Scientific American Library. Comprehensive book on the biology of rainforests; for education as well as travel purposes.

Tidwell, M.
1996 *Amazon Stranger: A Rainforest Chief Battles Big Oil.* New York: Lyons and Burford. The role of Randy Borman of Zábalo in excluding oil from the eastern Cuyabeno Wildlife Reserve.

Vickers, W.T.
1989 *Los Sionas y Secoyas, Su adaptación al Ambiente Amazónico.* Colección 500 Años. Quito: Ediciones Abya Yala.

Weiss, E.A.
1997 *A Comprehensive Guide to Wilderness and Travel Medicine.* Oakland, CA: Adventure Medical Kits. Practical pocket-size book on the explanations and treatments of tourist-related illnesses.

Wesche, R.
1993 Ecotourism and Indigenous Peoples in the Resource Frontier of the Ecuadorian Amazon. *Yearbook, Conference of Latin Americanist Geographers* 19: 35-45. Indigenous involvement

in ecotourism and the prospects of community controlled ecotourism in Napo province.
AT

1995   *The Ecotourist's Guide to the Ecuadorian Amazon: Napo Province.* Quito: CEPEIGE. Survey of ecotourism attractions and services with detailed maps of Ecuador's Napo region; some emphasis on indigenous community controlled ecotourism. Available: CEPEIGE, 3er piso, Instituto Geográfico Militar, Apartado 17-01-4173, Quito, tel. 541 200, fax. 509 122.
AT and LM

1996   Developed Country Environmentalism and Indigenous Community Controlled Ecotourism in the Ecuadorian Amazon. *Geographische Zeitschrift* 3&4: 157-168. Evolution of indigenous community controlled ecotourism in the Ecuadorian Amazon in response to changing influences of Western environmental and ecotourism organizations.
AT

Whitmore, T.C.
1992   A*n Introduction to Tropical Rain Forests.* New York: Oxford University Press. Mostly suited for advanced education and professional purposes.

Williams, R., Best, B. and Heijnen, T.
1997.   *A Guide to Bird-watching in Ecuador and the Galápagos Islands.* Biosphere Publications.
Comprehensive guide to bird-watching locations in Ecuador. Available: Bird Buteo Books, Box 242, Shipman, VA 22971 USA.
ABY and LM

Wunder, S.

1996 *Ecoturismo, Ingresos Locales y Conservación: El Caso de Cuyabeno, Ecuador.* Quito: Abya Yala. Extensive case studies on ecotourism in the Cuyabeno Wildlife Reserve covering economic, environmental and social aspects.
ABY

Yost, J.A.

1981 Twenty Years of Contact: The Mechanisms of Change in Wao ("Auca") Culture. In *Cultural Transformations and Ethnicity in Modern Ecuador,* ed. N.E. Whitten Jr., pp. 677-704. Urbana: University of Illinois Press. Describes the changes in Huaorani settlement and interaction patterns with an outline of the history of contacts with the colonist culture.
ABY (Spanish version).

1991 Los Waorani: Un Pueblo de la Selva. In *Ecuador a la Sombra de los Volcanes,* pp. 98-100; 107-108. Quito: Libri Mundi.

AA: Available at Acción Amazonía in Quito
           Av. República 307 y Almagro, Edificio Taurus, apto
           #1A Tel: (593-2) 225 907, 234 594
           E-mail: accionamazonia@ecuadorexplorer.com

ABY: Available at Abya Yala in Quito
           Av.Doce de Octubre 1430 y Wilson Tel: (539-2) 506
           247, 562 633

AT: Available from the Authors (see following page)

LM: Available at Libri Mundi in Quito
           Juan Leon Mera 8514 y Wilson Tel: (593-2) 529 587,
           234 791

TES: Available at The Ecotourism Society, PO Box 755,
           North Bennington, VT 05257, USA Tel: (802) 447 2121
           Fax: (802) 447 2122 E-mail: ecomail@ecotourism.org
           Internet: www.ecotourism.org

AUTHORS' ADDRESSES

Rolf Wesche
Environmental Studies, University of Ottawa
165 Waller St., P.O. Box 450, Stn. A
Ottawa, Ontario
K1N 6N5 Canada
(613) 562-5800 ext. 1040
Fax: (613) 562-5145
rwesche@aix1.uottawa.ca

Andy Drumm
Acción Amazonía
Av. República 307 y Almagro, Edif. Taurus
Quito, Ecuador
(593-2) 225 907, 234 594
Fax: (593-2) 560 756
adrumm@earthlink.com

CBE PROJECTS	MID / LOWER NAPO		SUCUMBIOS								
	Quehueire'ono	Añangu (current state)	Oyacachi	Zábalo	Playas de Cuyabeno	Siecoya	Sinangüé	Dureno	Puerto Bolívar	Biaña	Orahuëäyá
English speaking guides	**			**							
sleeping facilities	*	*	*	**	*	*	*	*	*	*	*
showers				*	*					*	*
flush toilet			*	*	*		*			*	*
latrines	*					*	*		*	*	
electricity			*	*							
camping	**		*				*				
boots provided					*		*				
easy access								*	**		
1 day program											
remote	**	**	*	**	**	*				*	
easy hiking	*	*		*	*	*	*		*	*	*
strenuous hiking	*		**	**		**		*			
free time	*	*	*	*	*	*	*		*	**	*
wildlife viewing	**	**		**	**	*	*		*	*	*
primary forest	**	*		**	**	*	*	*	**	*	*
waterfalls			**				*				
panoramic viewing point	*		**	*			**				
unexplored caves											
caves											
petroglyphs											
cultural program (dance/music)	*					*		*		*	*
handicraft production	**		**	**	*	*	*	*		*	
shamanic presentation						*					*
medicinal plant garden						**	*				
museum				*							
participation in minga											
canopy tower				*	**						
paddle canoeing	**	*		*	**		*	*	**	*	**
fishing	**	*	**	*	*	*	*		*	*	*
gold panning							*				
swimming	**	*		*	*	*	*	*	*	*	
lianas to swing on				*					**	**	

CBE PROJECTS	Kapawi	Pavacachi	Curaray	Llanchamacocha - Jandiayacu	Canelos - Sarayacu	Canelos	Chunchupamba	San Pedro	Fátima, Indi Churis, Hola Vida	Parque OMAERE	Sapallo	Huacamayos & AACLAC	Las Galeras	Chuva Urcu	Rio Blanco	San José de Puma Pungo	Salazar Aitaca	Capirona	Runa Huasi	Machacuyacu	Unión Venezia	Cuya Loma
						PASTAZA												UPPER NAPO				
English speaking guides	**																			**		
sleeping facilities	**	*	*	*	*	*	*	*		*		**	*	*	*	*		*	**	**	**	*
showers	**	*				*	*			*		**	*	*	*			*	**	**		*
flush toilet	**	*				*				*		**	*	*	*			*	**	**		*
latrines							*	*	*									*		*		
electricity	**					*	*			*		**						*				*
camping	*	*				*						**	**	*		*		*				
boots provided	**	*												*				*		*		
easy access							*	*	*	*	**	**						*		*	**	**
1 day program							*	*	**	*	*	*						*		*	*	**
remote	**	**	**	**	*									*	*	*		*		*		
easy hiking	*	*	*	*	*	*			*	*	*	*	*	*		*		*	*	*	*	*
strenuous hiking	*	*						*	*				*	**	*			**	*			
free time	*	*				*	*		**	**		*	*	*	*			*	**	*	**	*
wildlife viewing	**	**	*	**				*					*			*		*	*	**	*	
primary forest	**	**	*	**				*				*				*		*	*	**	*	
waterfalls			**	*	*	**		*			*	**	*	**				*	**	*	*	
panoramic viewing point						*		**	*			*	**	*				*			**	
unexplored caves									*			*	**					*			**	
caves												**	*	*				**	*	*		
petroglyphs											*	**						**				
cultural program (dance/music)		*				*				*		**	*	*	*	**	*	**		*	*	**
handicraft production	*									**		**	*	*	*			**		*	**	*
shamanic presentation			*						**						*	*		*				*
medicinal plant garden						*		*		*		**	*			**	*	*				
museum										**		*										**
participation in minga						*		*						*	*			*		*		
canopy tower																						
paddle canoeing	**		*		**							*		*				**		**		
fishing	**	*	*	**	*									*	*			*				
gold panning											*		*									
swimming	*					*				*	*	*	*	**	*	*		**	*	**		*
lianas to swing on									**	*			*					*				**

ANEXOS